D1444836

FOUNDATIONS OF PROGRAMMING WITH PASCAL

THE ELLIS HORWOOD SERIES IN
COMPUTERS AND THEIR APPLICATIONS

Series Editor: BRIAN MEEK
Computer Unit, Queen Elizabeth College, University of London

The series aims to provide up-to-date and readable texts on the theory and practice of computing, with particular though not exclusive emphasis on computer applications. Preference is given in planning the series to new or developing areas, or to new approaches in established areas.

The books will usually be at the level of introductory or advanced undergraduate courses. In most cases they will be suitable as course texts, with their use in industrial and commercial fields always kept in mind. Together they will provide a valuable nucleus for a computing science library.

Published and in active publication

INTERACTIVE COMPUTER GRAPHICS IN SCIENCE TEACHING
Edited by J. McKENZIE, University College, London, L. ELTON, University of Surrey, R. LEWIS, Chelsea College, London.

INTRODUCTORY ALGOL 68 PROGRAMMING
D. F. BRAILSFORD and A. N. WALKER, University of Nottingham.

GUIDE TO GOOD PROGRAMMING PRACTICE
Edited by B. L. MEEK, Queen Elizabeth College, London and P. HEATH, Plymouth Polytechnic.

DYNAMIC REGRESSION: Theory and Algorithms
L. J. SLATER and H. M. PESARAN, Trinity College, Cambridge.

CLUSTER ANALYSIS ALGORITHMS: For Data Reduction and Classification of Objects
H. SPÄTH, Professor of Mathematics, Oldenburg University.

FOUNDATIONS OF PROGRAMMING WITH PASCAL
LAWRIE MOORE, Birkbeck College, London.

RECURSIVE FUNCTIONS IN COMPUTER SCIENCE
R. PETER, formerly Eotvos Lorand University of Budapest.

SOFTWARE ENGINEERING
K. GEWALD, G. HAAKE and W. PFADLER

PROGRAMMING LANGUAGE STANDARDISATION
Edited by B. L. MEEK, Queen Elizabeth College, London and I. D. HILL, Clinical Research Centre, Harrow.

FUNDAMENTALS OF COMPUTER LOGIC
D. HUTCHISON, University of Strathclyde.

SYSTEMS ANALYSIS AND DESIGN FOR COMPUTER APPLICATION
D. MILLINGTON, University of Strathclyde.

ADA: A PROGRAMMER'S CONVERSION COURSE
M. J. STRATFORD-COLLINS, U.S.A.

A COURSE IN COMPUTER SCIENCE
B. L. MEEK, Queen Elizabeth College, London, S. FAIRTHORNE, Queen Elizabeth College, London, P. WESTON, Bangor Technical College and P. MYERS, John Fisher School, Croydon.

FOUNDATIONS OF PROGRAMMING WITH PASCAL

LAWRIE MOORE, M.Phil.
Head of Computing Services
Birkbeck College
University of London

ELLIS HORWOOD LIMITED
Publishers · Chichester

Halsted Press: a division of
JOHN WILEY & SONS
New York · Chichester · Brisbane · Toronto

First published in 1980 by

ELLIS HORWOOD LIMITED
Market Cross House, Cooper Street, Chichester, West Sussex, PO19 1EB, England

*The publisher's colophon is reproduced from James Gillison's drawing of the
ancient Market Cross, Chichester.*

Distributors:

Australia, New Zealand, South-east Asia:
Jacaranda-Wiley Ltd., Jacaranda Press,
JOHN WILEY & SONS INC.,
G.P.O. Box 859, Brisbane, Queensland 40001, Australia.

Canada:
JOHN WILEY & SONS CANADA LIMITED
22 Worcester Road, Rexdale, Ontario, Canada.

Europe, Africa:
JOHN WILEY & SONS LIMITED
Baffins Lane, Chichester, West Sussex, England.

North and South America and the rest of the world:
Halsted Press: a division of
JOHN WILEY & SONS
605 Third Avenue, New York, N.Y. 10016, U.S.A.

British Library Cataloguing in Publication Data
Moore, Lawrie
    Foundations of programming with Pascal. —
    (Ellis Horwood series in computers and their applications).
    1. PASCAL (Computer program language)
    I. Title
    001.6'424   QA76.73.P2   80-40146
ISBN 0-85312-171-0 (Ellis Horwood Ltd., Publishers, Library Edition)
ISBN 0-470-26939-1 (Halsted Press)

Typeset in Press Roman by Ellis Horwood Ltd.
Printed in Great Britain by W & J Mackay Ltd., Chatham

Table of Contents

10 **Table of Contents**

Preface

'It is important that students bring a certain ragamuffin, barefoot irreverance to their studies; they are here not to worship what is known but to question it.'
Jacob Bronowski

This book is about programming. The fact that it introduces the programming language Pascal is less important than what it has to say about programming itself. It is only natural, in a book intended for beginners, to choose Pascal as the programming language to teach, because Pascal is, without any doubt, the language which has won first place as the introductory teaching language of computer science. This is because it provides the means of expressing in simple and lucid terms all the more important constructions which, in other languages, can be expressed only clumsily, inelegantly, or in a way which is difficult to understand.

Nevertheless, there is a great difference between learning a language and learning the basic concepts of programming. Very often the latter is deferred, either until some time after the student has learnt one or more languages and many bad habits, or forever. The purpose of this book is to provide a first course in programming for anyone who wants to learn how to do it properly; it should be a suitable text for use in any introductory course in universities, polytechnics and other institutions of higher education, or for self-study.

Because it is a textbook, the presentation of material follows the chronological order in which it is pedagogically required, the introduction of new material being deferred until needed. The result is that the order of presentation differs from many other textbooks which attempt either to compromise or to serve as a reference manual for the programming language being introduced.

Not only is it considered a mistake for a textbook to try to supplant a reference manual: part of the task of a student programmer is to learn how to read and understand the (more difficult) reference manual. The reference manual for Pascal is entitled 'Pascal User Manual and Report' by Kathleen Jensen and Niklaus Wirth, published by Springer-Verlag, and every serious user of Pascal should refer to it.

The material introduced in this textbook has sought, on the whole, to avoid any mathematics which would be unfamiliar to non-specialists in mathematics. An exception is made in Chapter 15, which deals with numerical integration.

This application of computing often arises as a practical problem precisely for non-mathematicians. It is generally dealt with in advanced texts, whose treatment is theoretical and difficult for the non-specialist to follow. Chapter 15, by contrast, provides the mathematical know-how required for practical integration, and uses it in illustrating some advanced programming techniques which result in simple, flexible and powerful programs. Moreover, this exercise is felt to be a realistic demonstration of what can be done by passing a function as a parameter to another function which is called recursively.

There is no attempt to cover every single feature of the Pascal language, and this is no part of the purpose of the book. In particular, it may be noticed that, apart from its occurrence in the complete syntax of the language provided in an appendix, there is no mention of the **goto**. No apology is made for this omission. It is felt that the **goto** serves no useful purpose, and has some harmful effects, in an elementary introduction to programming in a high-level language.

The syntax definition of Pascal is presented in two forms: the syntax diagrams as used in the Report, and a new style BNF which follows the preliminary proposals made by a Working Group on Syntactic Metalanguages (BSI Committee DPS/13) in their paper issued in 1979, *The need for a standard.* Chapter 6, *Waving the rules*, has been devoted to introducing these syntax notations in order to make it easier for the student to refer to the Pascal Revised Report and to other language definitions. Appendices give Pascal syntax both in the form of diagrams and in the BSI Working Group proposal's new-style BNF.

There are thought provoking problems provided at the end of each chapter. Answering these provides the student with the opportunity for reinforcement of understanding by putting it to work, the surest way of learning. A set of solutions is not specifically provided. This is because either the solutions are factual and the required information is already in the text, or the problems exercise the readers' conceptual understanding, in which case their value lies in the doing and not in the solution.

I have received encouragement, criticism and other valuable help from many colleagues and friends, and from my family. Thanks are due to all of them, but in particular to the series editor, Brian Meek.

CHAPTER 1

Very basic concepts

This excellent machine is neatly planned,
A child, a half-wit would not feel perplexed:
No chance to err, you simply press the button –
At once each cog in motion moves the next.

John Lehmann

1.1 INTRODUCTION

This book assumes no previous knowledge of computing or programming. Starting from scratch, a theoretical and practical foundation is laid, providing a sound basis both for those who wish to become specialists, and for those who, while interested in computing only as a tool, prefer to understand the tool rather than rely upon a cook-book. By analogy, an elementary knowledge of the basic processes going on under the bonnet and chassis of a car provides a sound basis for understanding what the various controls do; surely this is a desirable part of learning to drive a car, as well as being necessary for the intending automobile engineer.

Like the automobile, the computer is a machine. Writers of science fiction have replaced this mere machine by a myth possessing magical qualities which are within our imagination, but beyond our comprehension. But the computer is no magical myth; it is, increasingly, a machine which plays an integral part in almost every facet of everyday life.

There is a sound reason for this. Our age has produced the greatest information explosion the world has seen; and the computer is a machine for processing information. What does it mean to process information? First of all, let us notice what it does not mean. It does not mean thinking. The computer is not a brain. It does not create but simply carries out processes upon information to which it has access, and then outputs the results. The processes it can carry out may be, for example, to rearrange the information in some way, or to output selections from the supplied information, or to change the way in which the information is represented and output it using the new changed representation.

Of course, the computer cannot process information directly, because information is something abstract, and a machine cannot process abstractions. Beauty, it is said, is in the eye of the beholder – and perhaps, also, in the mind of an artist. Information, too, exists in the minds of the communicator and the receiver of the information. Somehow, it is transmitted from the one to the other, but how? This printed page is not in itself information, but merely ink marks upon a white sheet. The ink marks are a coded representation of the information which is to be transmitted. Exactly the same information could be transmitted quite differently in many ways, for example in morse code, or in Chinese, or in Braille. Another method would be to use a code which represents each graphic character on the page by an associated pattern of holes punched in a card. We distinguish any particular representation (of a piece of information) from the information it represents by calling it 'data'. The way we use computers to process information is that first we represent the information by some form of data. Correctly speaking, it is the data (and not the information) which is stored in the computer, and what the computer does is data-processing. The data output from the computer conveys to our minds the processed information which is represented.

We have characterised the computer as a machine which processes data. An integral part of the computer which enables it to perform this task on a grand scale is its memory, or store, as it is also called. Data may be put into store by any of the processes carried out by the computer. One of the most important from a practical point of view is that known as data input. This process enables data to be 'input' to the machine, for example transferred via a peripheral device such as a punched card reader, and stored in the computer memory in an organised way so that it may be retrieved and operated upon by other processes. Some processes may themselves generate data values, which they put directly into store.

Any process which we require the computer to carry out must be specified to it in a very definite manner. Indeed, special formal 'languages' have been devised especially for this purpose. They are called programming languages. Like natural languages, each has its own vocabulary, its own grammar, and its own set of rules which defines the exact meaning of statements and expressions in the language. Most of these programming languages bear some similarities to the language of mathematics and logic, because they are used to describe or prescribe operations to be carried out upon data values. A data value may be a numerical quantity, or some non-numerical value such as a colour or stock classification code. It may be a chunk of textual information such as a word or sentence, or a chapter of a book; it may be a record, that is, a collection of items, each item being a value related to the whole record in some way.

In order to describe operations to be carried out upon data values, it is common, in the language of mathematics, to talk about variables, and about constants, and most people who have even a small acquaintance with mathematics have a general idea of what is a variable, and what is a constant. Such vague general ideas may suffice up to a point, at least when talking to human beings, who have a remarkable facility (sometimes called intelligence) for understanding what you mean even when you may not express your ideas very clearly. Talking to human beings is one thing, but talking to machines (computers) is quite something else. A machine has neither brain nor intelligence; it has merely a set of automatic responses to the stimuli it receives. It reacts in exactly the same manner if you flick a particular control switch with calculated intention as it does if you brush accidentally and unintentionally against the switch. A human being is cleverer than that, but not so obedient. It is necessary therefore to examine much more closely the exact meaning of technical terms like 'constant', 'variable', 'process', and others, and to understand the way in which they are used in the language of mathematics, and of computing.

In order to be able to discuss the form and meaning of the language we are going to study, we must therefore introduce definitions of technical terms we shall use, forgetting any preconceived ideas we had about the meaning of these terms.

1.2 NAMES, VALUES AND CONSTANTS

The property which semantically defines a *constant* is that it *denotes* (that is, *names*) some particular thing. It is most important to distinguish between the name of an object and the object itself. In English we use quotation marks for this purpose.

Compare the sentences:

(i) I am John Smith.
(ii) My name is 'John Smith'.

These are both meaningful sentences. However, the following two sentences do not make sense at all:

(iii) I am 'John Smith'.
(iv) My name is John Smith.

The 'I' in (iii) is implied to be not a person but a string of letters, while (iv) states that my name is a person called John Smith. 'John Smith' is a *constant*. John Smith is a person denoted by that constant.

Some confusion arises when we turn our attention to numbers, partly because the name of a number and the number itself are both of them abstract concepts, and are therefore less obviously distinguishable than John Smith and 'John Smith'. A number is a value, but a constant is a name which denotes that value. The names: 'IV', 'FOUR', '4' are *constants*. Each of them denotes the same object, which is the value 4. We see that the number itself is a value and not a constant.

The sentences (v), (vi) and (vii) make sense:

(v) Three times five is fifteen.
(vi) Five differs from 3 by two.
(vii) 'Five' begins with the letter 'F'.

The sentences (viii), (ix) and (x) and (xi) do not:

  (viii) Three times 'five' is fifteen.
   (ix)   'Five' differs from '3' by two.
    (x)   Five begins with the letter, 'F'.
   (xi)   Five has four letters.

Note the difference in meaning between

   (xii) 'John' has four letters.
and
  (xiii) John has four letters.

1.3 VARIABLES

We have seen that the expression 'a number' is not a constant because it is not a name denoting a particular value − but it may be used to talk about numbers in general. We may say for example: 'If we multiply a number by itself we obtain its square'. If we want to obtain the square of a particular number, we must substitute a constant which denotes that number for 'a number'. The expression 'a number' is used here as a *variable*.

A variable does not denote a particular value. It is associated with a set of values called its *domain*. Any constant which denotes one of these values may be substituted for the variable. The variable is merely a place-holder for such a constant. That is to say, a variable is a reserved space which may be occupied by any one of a set of values. Its place may be taken by a constant denoting one of these values. (The role of a variable is well illustrated by a piece of hand-luggage deposited upon a railway-carriage seat, where it is a place-holder for a traveller). The particular *domain* of values associated with a variable is denoted by the *type* of the variable. For example we might say:

   ' "n" is a variable of type integer'.
   ' "x" is a variable of type real'.

In the examples given, the domain of n is the set of all integers, while the domain of x is the set of all reals, and this is denoted by the phrases 'of type integer', and 'of type real'. Substituting a constant for a variable is illegal if the value denoted by the constant is of incorrect type, that is to say, if it does not belong to the *domain* of values of the variable.

It is therefore necessary, when writing an expression containing a variable, to *specify* the type of the variable, for example, $f(x) = x^2 + 2x + 1$, for real x, defines the value $f(x)$ for all real values which may be substituted for x but leaves the value undefined in a case where a substitution does not denote a real value. Substitution of a constant denoting a value belonging to the domain of the variable is called a *legal* substitution.

We carry over into computing the linguistic concepts of mathematics which have been described; but some of them are extended and enriched, whilst others are changed. This is not because the mathematical concepts are wrong, or that the computing concepts are better. It is because the mathematical concepts have been generalised to a form which facilitates mathematical manipulation. The mathematician requires a mathematical model which he can study and with which he can do mathematical experiments. In computing we require a different kind of model, suited to the manipulations and experiments which can be carried out on computers.

1.4 VARIABLES AND CONSTANTS IN COMPUTER PROGRAMS

We have already said that, unlike a *constant*, a *variable* does not denote a particular value, but is a place-holder for a *constant* which belongs to the *domain* of values with which the *variable* is associated. We call this *domain* the *type* of the *variable*. In a mathematical sense, the foregoing definition may seem to be an abstract concept; but in computing, this definition becomes a physical reality.

(i) The place-holder is a particular cell of the computer memory or store.

(ii) The *name* of the *variable* denotes that store-cell. It is a synonym for the address of the store-cell.

(iii) We can make a legal substitution for the variable by storing a particular constant in that store-cell.

(iv) The constant we store in the store-cell denoted by the *name* of the variable must be of suitable *type*. (Its value must belong to the *domain* of the variable).

These ideas are fairly straightforward, but they introduce new levels of complexity which may cause misunderstanding. We have said that a constant denotes a particular object. Note that we are now talking about the *name* of a *variable* denoting a store-cell. This means that the *name* of a *variable* is a *constant*.

This constant denotes a particular store-cell inside the computer. The actual address of the store-cell need not concern us provided the computer associates that store-cell with the name of the variable whenever we use it.

1.5 THE ASSIGNMENT OPERATION

QUESTION: When do we want to use the *name* of a variable (as distinct from using the variable itself)?

ANSWER: When we want to say for example, 'Substitute for "x" the value 3.1'.

In this answer we are clearly using the *name* of x, and that is why it is in quotes. In many computer programming languages, if we wish to make a substitution, we write:

$x := 3.1$

we mean by this

'x' takes the value 3.1

but the quotes round x are omitted, for we know that it is being used as the name of a store-cell because it is followed by the assignment symbol ':='. However, we may also write

$x := y$

where x and y are both variables of the same type. Now we have already seen that:

(i) a variable does not denote a value, but is associated with a set of values.

(ii) a variable on the left of an assignment symbol actually signifies the name of the variable, that is, it is being used as a name constant which denotes the store cell of that name.

(iii) An assignment is nothing more than the legal substitution of a constant of suitable type for a variable. Hence the expression on the right of an assignment symbol must be a constant. It therefore seems that the variable y in the assignment above is a constant! This is a contradiction.

Certainly y is a variable at the time when the assignment statement is being written or read. But when the program runs, and the computing machine is actually carrying out the assignment, a constant is required on the right hand side of the assignment-symbol where 'y' is written. This constant is obtained by 'evaluating' the right hand side, that is by taking as a legal substitution for 'y' the value which is stored in its store-cell.

Perhaps we can now paraphrase the assignment statement $x := y$ as:

'x' := (the last legal substitution which was made for y)

or

put in the store-cell called 'x' a copy of the current contents of the store-cell called 'y'.

In short, we may regard the assignment symbol ':=', as an operator which forces substitution of a value for the expression which follows it. This exercise of forcing substitution of a value is known as evaluation of the expression, and is followed by subsequent assignment of that value to the variable preceding the assignment symbol.

1.6 ALGORITHMS

The word *algorithm* derives from the name of the ninth-century Persian mathematician, Abu Ja'far Mohammed ibn Musa al-Kuwarizmi, which means 'father of Ja'far, Mohammed, son of Moses, native of Kuwarizmi', and has come down to us through centuries of western culture as Al-Kuwarizmi and thence via Algorithmus to Algorithm. Mathematics has not stood still since the ninth century, and the meaning of the word Algorithm has changed accordingly; but it appears always to have been used to describe processes of computation, for example, the processes which must be followed in carrying out the arithmetical operations of addition, subtraction, multiplication, or division. In the computer age its meaning has been generalised to denote any process which is carried out according to a set of sequential instructions, irrespective of whether the process is computational or otherwise. At the same time, its meaning has been refined to the precision of a technical term which narrows its proper use as we shall see. Every algorithm has two essential characteristics:

(i) An algorithm is sequential.
(ii) An algorithm is finite.

There is a great difference between an algorithm and a formula. For example, the roots of a quadratic equation with coefficients a, b, c, are given by the following formula:

$$x = \frac{-b \pm \sqrt{(b^2 - 4ac)}}{2a}.$$

An algorithm corresponding to this formula might be written as a sequence of steps as follows:

1. Find the value of $(b^2 - 4ac)$ and call it D.
2. Find the square root of D (whether real or imaginary) and call it S.
3. Subtract S from $(-b$ and call it U.
4. Subtract b from S and call it V.
5. Divide U by $2a$ and call it $R1$.
6. Divide V by $2a$ and call it $R2$.
7. $R1$ and $R2$ are the required roots.

In the case of the example given, the difference between the algorithm and the formula to which it corresponds is quite genuine if the calculation is to be done upon a simple pocket calculator. However, in a very sophisticated computer programming language, we might be able to write:

1. Evaluate $(-b + \sqrt{(b^2 - 4ac)})/2a$ and call it $R1$.
2. Evaluate $(-b - \sqrt{(b^2 - 4ac)})/2a$ and call it $R2$.
3. Print the values of $R1$ and $R2$.

This algorithm is much closer to the actual formula, but the essential difference remains. An algorithm is characterised by the fact that it consists of a *sequence* of *instructions*. The instructions are carried out in the prescribed order.

This means that during the course of executing an algorithm, the value of a particular variable may be changed. At any one instant of time, between consecutive instructions, that variable has one and only one value, namely the value last assigned to it. It may be noticed that the register of a calculator behaves in precisely the same way.

The other important characteristic of an algorithm is that it can be proved to terminate in a definite number of steps. The termination may either yield the required result, or it may yield an answer giving the information that no result could be found.

1.7 COMPUTER PROGRAMS

A computer program may be regarded as an algorithm written in a form suitable for presenting to a computer for its execution. A program has therefore all the characteristics of an algorithm which have been mentioned. Since it is suitable for presentation to a machine, it must be not only precise and unambiguous, but also be composed from basic instructions (or steps) which the machine has been constructed to accept and act upon.

It must in fact be written in some particular programming language. Such a language, unlike a natural language, is formally and precisely defined. Its definition must include:

(i) VOCABULARY. This is the set of symbols permitted for use in constructing valid statements in the language.

(ii) GRAMMAR. This is a set of rules which must be observed when stringing symbols together to form valid statements in the language.

(iii) SEMANTICS. This is a set of rules which determine (hopefully utterly unambiguously) the meaning (or lack of meaning) of any valid statement in the language.

The programs studied in this book are written in the programming language 'Pascal' (named after the seventeenth-century French mathematician, Blaise Pascal, who was born in 1623 and died in 1662).

1.8 DATA STORAGE

In order that data may have processing operations carried out upon it by a computer, the data must be accessible to the processor unit of the computer, that is, to that part of the computer which carries out the processing. Being 'accessible' means that the data must be recorded on some medium by data-recording devices which may be regarded as part of the computer system, there being other devices for 'reading' what is recorded. There are storage devices of many different kinds, but the most important difference is that between 'random-access' and 'sequential-access' devices.

What is meant by random access and sequential access? Let us take an example from outside the computing scene which will illustrate each access-mode. Consider two 'books'. One is a dictionary, produced in the normal twentieth-century manner, that is, on printed pages bound together. The other is a geometry book of Euclid's theorems, produced, say, in mediaeval times, written in the form of a scroll which, wound around a former (or spool), may be unwound, read, and wound onto a second former or spool as the reading continues. When the entire scroll has been read, it is completely unwound from the first spool and completely wound up onto the second spool. Before it may be read again from the beginning, it must be rewound. The only way in which such a scroll may be read (or written) is sequentially. By contrast, the dictionary may be flipped open at any required page at random. The paged, bound book is a random-access device, whilst the spooled scroll is a sequential-access device. Of course, the random-access book did not have to be a dictionary; this idea was introduced merely to make the example more understandable — after all, we do require random access to a dictionary; a sequential-access dictionary (say of the size of the twenty-four volume Oxford dictionary) would be extremely inconvenient, if not unusable.

A more up-to-date example of a sequential-access device for data-storage is a (musical) tape-recorder. It is more up-to-date, because both the mode of *putting* (recording) data into storage, and the mode of *getting* (playing-back) data from storage, use electro-magnetic technology, which was not available in the days of quill pen and parchment. However, from our present point of view, this distinction is quite superficial, because there is an astonishing similarity if not identity in type of access-mode between the modern tape-recorder and the mediaeval scroll. They are both sequential-access devices.

The modern computer uses data-storage devices of both main types, sequential-access and random-access. That type of store providing random-access in the most direct manner is variously called 'central memory', 'core-store', 'core memory', or sometimes simply 'memory'. There also exist types of storage-device which, in a sense, lie somewhere between the two main types, since they provide random access to rather large blocks of data, and these blocks may be put or got only as entire chunks. However, we are concerned mainly with the fundamental types, sequential and random.

The central memory may be thought of as a large collection of individual storage locations, rather like pigeon-holes, each of which may be used to store a data-value of some kind. Any particular pigeon-hole may be accessed at any time, either for putting or getting data. Furthermore, we may access any set of these pigeon-holes, wherever each may be situated in central memory, in any order we choose. This is what constitutes random-access.

In a high-level programming language like Pascal, we refer to the individual locations in random-access memory by giving them names which we invent for our own convenience and which we choose in a way which makes our program logical and easier to understand. There are grammatical rules governing the form of these names. Names formed in the correct manner according to the rules are called identifiers. The rules in Pascal are as follows:

RULES FOR FORMING IDENTIFIERS
A valid identifier must start with a letter. It may either consist of only one letter, or this letter may be followed by any number of characters, each of which is either a letter or a digit. No characters other than letters or digits are permitted in valid identifiers.

Examples of valid identifiers in Pascal (separated by commas)

> $x, u, w, salary, fred, amount3,$
> $a3b1c, temp, voltage, cat, xray,$
> $xsquared, ysqud, phi, theta, sigma, one,$
> $two, three47, sevenx.$

Examples of invalid identifiers in Pascal (separated by commas)

> $2, 4by, new\ x, old\ y, area-3, man.height,$
> $max/vol, pounds*.$

The programmer in a high-level language does not need to know (or keep track of) which locations in (random-access) store he is using, because the machine does this for him. He does need to 'tell' the machine:

(i) the identifier he proposes to use for referring to each particular variable in the program;

(ii) the type of value which will be stored in the store-location denoted by the identifier for each of these variables.

The passing of this information to the machine, although part of the program, does not form part of the 'action' of the program, but is rather a *description* of the data upon which the program is to operate. It is part of the organisation required before the actions of the program may begin. This preparatory part of the program is known as the 'declaration' part. Every constant and every variable to be used in the program must be 'declared', and the way in which this is done must, of course, conform to the grammatical rules of the programming language.

In Pascal, a variable declaration has three parts:

(i) the word '**var**';

(ii) an identifier (or a list of identifiers for variables of the same type);

(iii) the type.

Examples: **var** *count* : *integer*
              var *j, k, cases* : *integer*

Note: that 'var' is separated from the identifier list by at least one space;
         that the identifiers in the list are separated by commas;
         that the identifier list is separated from the type part of the declaration by a colon.

For improving the clarity of meaning of a declaration, it is recommended that it should always be read, whether aloud or mentally, (in the above examples) as:

   (i) Variable *count*, of type *integer*.
  (ii) Variables *j, k, cases*, of type *integer*.

The declaration part of a computer program constitutes a 'description' of the data to be processed by the program. It is not concerned with the actions to be taken by the program in the course of processing the data.

1.9 ABSTRACT MODEL OF A COMPUTING SYSTEM

The way in which a computer behaves may be studied at a number of different levels. At a low level, we should be concerned with the characteristics of transistors, coils, capacitors, resistors and other electronic components, and their behaviour when linked together in electronic circuits; or alternatively, with the behaviour characteristics of equivalent integrated-circuit chips. We could go to an even lower level, and study the physico-chemical behaviour of the materials of which these components are made. At a higher level, we could study logical circuits and the logical diagrams embodying the design of the machine, the construction of its memory and how this is organised, and the built-in functions of which the machine is capable. These functions are very primitive, or elementary, such as copying a binary pattern from one part of memory to another. At this level, even a simple operation like adding two numbers together may require a sequence of several basic machine-orders, each of which is the application of one of the primitive functions, or machine-instructions, of the computer.

However, we shall not be concerned directly with such low-level points of view, but rather with the characteristics of the system, as it appears in general to behave, from the point of view of a programmer in a high-level programming language, and in particular when that language is Pascal. Such a generalised abstract model gives the essential characteristics of the computer, and these may be summarised as follows:

   (i) A (direct random-access) memory, capable of storing a large number of values.
  (ii) A set of functions for changing the state of the memory. These are the functions (instructions) used to process the data.

(iii) At least one function (or set of functions) which can be used to 'get' data from a sequential-access device. This is required for data input.

(iv) At least one function which can be used to 'put' data to a sequential-access device. This is required for data output.

(v) A stored program of instructions to be obeyed in sequence.

(vi) A built-in pre-programmed routine for responding to a Pascal computer program, by arranging its data-storage (as required by the program declarations), and carrying out the actions (as required by the program instructions).

1.10 PROBLEMS

1.10.1

State which of the following sentences are grammatically correct, and meaningful, giving reasons:

(i) Eskimo Nell is a beautiful name.

(ii) 'Eskimo Nell' is a beautiful person.

(iii) Euclidean geometry started with Euclid.

(iv) 'Euclidean geometry' starts with 'Euclid'.

(v) The telegram I am holding contains ten words, but 'the telegram I am holding' contains five words.

(vi) Ten is greater than nine, and 'nine-tenths' is greater than 'nine'.

1.10.2

A set of instructions for calculating weekly wages contains the following statements (among others):

'1 is gross wage.
2 is total deductions.
3 is net wage.
$3 = 1 - 2$.'

Is the last statement nonsense or merely ambiguous? How can these statements be changed so that the meaning is clearly and correctly stated?

1.10.3

We say an integer n is *prime* if $n > 1$ and has no factors. The integer j is a factor of n if there is another integer k such that both are greater than 1 and less than n, and j times k is equal to n. (j may be equal to k). Describe how you would determine whether a given integer is prime. Is your answer an algorithm?

1.10.4

What is the name of my favourite day of the week? (I call it 'myday', to rhyme with 'friday'). Actually it rhymes with the name of the day which precedes it.

1.10.5

Delete and amend as necessary the essential characteristics (numbered (i) to (vi) in Section 1.9) of a Pascal computing system, so as to produce an abstract description, along similar lines, of an electronic pocket-calculator.

CHAPTER 2

Binary representation of data in storage

'Can you do addition?' The White Queen asked. 'What's one and one and one and one and one and one and one and one and one and one?' 'I don't know,' said Alice. 'I lost count.' 'She can't do addition,' the Red Queen interrupted.

Lewis Carroll

2.1 REPRESENTATION OF NUMBERS

2.1.1 Floating point numbers

Consider arithmetic values. These may be integers, such as $0, 1, 17, 64, 825706$, -53, etc., or they may be real numbers such as $3.14159, 27.2, 43000000$. When we perform calculations, we may find that the range of real numbers entering into the calculation is very large, and we then resort to a representation such as 3.1×10^{10}, 2.657×10^{17}, -1.3×10^{21}. This is called *floating point representation*, and is a most convenient way to represent any one of a set of real numbers expressed to an accuracy of a fixed number of digits, when the range of values is very wide. The representation used in $27.2, 3.14159$ is called *fixed point representation*.

If an individual storage location has space for storing only a fixed number of digits, it is clearly convenient to use the ideas behind floating point representation when storing real numbers. In fact it is only necessary to store the two parts 2613 and -27 of the value 2613×10^{-27} since the position of the decimal point is known, and the value of the exponent base is also known (in this case ten).

Even though we may know the contents of a storage location, we cannot know the value it represents unless we know the *type* of the value it represents.

An example is given of four different possible ways of storing the value 2.613×10^{-27}, using say six digit positions and two sign positions:

+	2	6	1	3	−	2	7
−	2	7	+	2	6	1	3
+	−	2	6	1	3	2	7
2	6	1	3	+	−	2	7

In the case of storage representation for integer values, a totally different pattern may be used, for example:

+	0	0	5	7	0	6	0

whereas a floating point number having an equal value might be represented quite differently, for example:

+	5	7	0	6	+	0	1

These storage patterns are quite arbitrary. The reason we are concerned at all, is in order to understand that when we invent an identifer for a variable, we must tell the machine what type of value it will have. For example in Pascal:

> **var** *j, k, counter*1, *counter*2 : *integer*;
> *average, sum, mass, height* : *real*;

These are Pascal *declarations*. They tell the machine to allocate storage locations to be used to store values of the type stated, and give the identifiers to be used to refer to these locations.

> A variable declaration does *not* put a value in a storage location; it obtains a location, gives it a name and declares its type.

The operation of putting a value into a storage location is effected by a Pascal statement called an *assignment* statement.

2.1.2 Representation of integers using the binary system

In everyday human practice, number are represented in a system called the *denary* (or decimal) system, based upon the number ten. (The same word root as 'denary' occurs with thirteen, fourteen, fifteen, etc., in the ending 'teen'). Most computers represent numbers using the *binary* system, based upon the number two. In the denary system, the digits zero through nine occur. In the binary system, only the digits zero and one occur.

In order to make clear some of the results of repesenting numbers inside computers as binary numbers, we shall consider two kinds of representation commonly used, and describe how to convert to or from denary, both for integers (whole numbers) and fractions (numbers less than one). The representations we describe do not necessarily refer to any particular computer, but are typical. For simplicity, we shall consider a very small number-range, zero through fifteen. This range requires only four bits in the binary system. ('bit' is a universally used abbreviated form of 'binary digit').

2.1.3 Negative integers

Table 2.1 shows straight binary values; but in order to provide a convenient way of representing signed values (positive or negative) a convention is used. The convention is based upon the fact that we have a finite range of numbers, because the memory inside the computer is physically limited, and hence each memory location can hold only a finite, definite number of bits. Using the 'two's complement' convention, we get a new table (see Table 2.2).

Table 2.1 — Binary–denary correspondence.

Denary	4-bit binary	Denary	4-bit binary
0	0000	8	1000
1	0001	9	1001
2	0010	10	1010
3	0011	11	1011
4	0100	12	1100
5	0101	13	1101
6	0110	14	1110
7	0111	15	1111

Table 2.2 — Correspondence using 2's complement.

Denary	4-bit binary	Denary	4-bit binary
0	0000	−8	1000
1	0001	−7	1001
2	0010	−6	1010
3	0011	−5	1011
4	0100	−4	1100
5	0101	−3	1101
6	0110	−2	1110
7	0111	−1	1111

Table 2.2 is best understood if the values are arranged around a clock face, and the counting mechanism is viewed as a rotary one, which repeats around the clock if there is 'overflow', that is, if the range is exceeded (see Fig. 2.1).

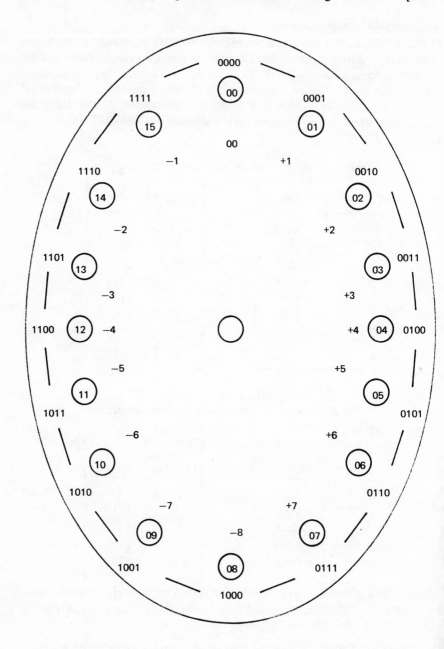

Fig. 2.1 – The two's complement clock (4-bit wordlength).

EXAMPLES OF ADDITION

(i)	Denary	Binary
	+3	0011
	−6	1010
	−3	1101

(ii)	−4	1100
	+4	0100
	0	0000

Note: The 'carry bit' is discarded (because there is no column to carry it to).

(iii)	−8	1000
	+7	0111
	−1	1111

If we attempt to carry out an operation which leads to a result outside the range of our system, we get 'overflow', and an incorrect result, for example:

	+2	0010	
	+7	0111	
	+9	1001	−7

NEGATION OF A NUMBER (for example, finding the 2's complement)

QUESTION: Suppose we know that +7 is 0111, how (without Table 2.2) do we find −7?

ANSWER: Subtract 0111 from 0000:

$$\begin{array}{r} 0000 \\ \text{less } 0111 \\ \hline 1001 \end{array}$$

Note: There is 1 to borrow at the end, and even though there is nowhere to borrow it from, a 1 is borrowed. The same result is obtained if a circular counting device is used.

An easier, though mechanical, way of finding the negative of a binary number is to change all 1s to 0s and 0s to 1s, and then add 1. This method may be checked by comparing the result it gives with the result obtained by subtraction from zero. The two results will always be identical.

2.2 CONVERSION FROM ONE BASE TO ANOTHER

2.2.1 To convert a denary integer to a binary integer

The method is to divide by 2 repeatedly. The remainder on each division (1 or 0)
is used to build the required answer, starting with the least significant bit. For
example, convert 323 to binary:

```
2)323    remainder
2)161         1
2) 80         1
2) 40        0
2) 20       0
2) 10      0
2)  5     0
2)  2    1
2)  1   0
    0  1
```

Result is 101000011.

2.2.2 To convert a binary integer to a denary integer

This method is analogous to the method once taught for converting say pounds,
shillings and pence to pence, but the arithmetic is easier, because the conversion involves multiplication only by 2. For example, convert 101000011 to
denary:

```
            101000011
        1    1
    X   2
      ─────
        2
    +   0    0
      ─────
        2
    X   2
      ─────
        4
    +   1    1
      ─────
        5
    X   2
      ─────
       10
    +   0    0
      ─────
       10
    X   2
      ─────
       20
```

```
                101000011
  +   0           0
  ───────
     20
  X   2
  ───────
     40
  +   0           0
  ───────
     40
  X   2
  ───────
     80
  +   0           0
  ───────
     80
  X   2
  ───────
    160
  +   1           1
  ───────
    161
  X   2
  ───────
    322
  +   1           1
  ───────
    323
```

Result is 323.

2.2.3 To convert a denary fraction (decimal) to binary

The method is to multiply the decimal fraction by 2 repeatedly. If an integer
part results, then a 1 goes into the answer, otherwise a zero. For example:

(i) Convert 0.1 decimal to binary;

```
                        0.1
                     X    2
                     ───────
                        0.2    0
                     X    2
                     ───────
                        0.4    0
                     X    2
                     ───────
                        0.8    0
                     X    2
                     ───────
                        1.6    1
                     X    2
                     ───────
                        1.2    1
```

So far, we have .00011.

The result is clearly non-terminating, that is, a recurring binary fraction 0.0 0011, or 0.0 followed by infinite repetition of the four bits 0011.

(ii) Convert .125 to binary. (We know this will convert to an exact binary fraction because one eighth is a power of 2);

$$
\begin{array}{ll}
.125 & \\
\times\ \ 2 & \\
\hline
.25 & 0 \\
\times\ \ 2 & \\
\hline
.5 & 0 \\
\times\ \ 2 & \\
\hline
1.0 & 1
\end{array}
$$

Result is the binary fraction .001.

2.2.4 To convert a binary fraction to a decimal fraction

First multiply by the smallest power of 2 necessary to convert the fraction to an integer; then convert the binary integer to a denary integer, we have already seen how to do that; and, lastly, divide (in denary) by the power of 2 used to multiply in the first step. For example:

(i) Convert .001 binary to decimal;

    step 1: multiply by 2 cubed (8)
           result is 1
    step 2: denary equivalent of binary 1 is 1
    step 3: denary 1 divided by 8 is .125.

(ii) Convert .111 binary to decimal (*note*: we know that .111 binary is a half plus a quarter plus an eighth so the result ought to be .875);

    step 1: multiply by 2 cubed
           result is 111

    step 2: convert to denary

$$
\begin{array}{cc}
 & 111 \\
1 & 1 \\
\times\ 2 & \\
\hline
2 &
\end{array}
$$

$$
\begin{array}{r r}
 & 111 \\
+\ 1 & \quad 1 \\
\hline
3 & \\
\times\ 2 & \\
\hline
6 & \\
+\ 1 & \quad 1 \\
\hline
7 & \\
\hline
\end{array}
$$

result is 7

step 3: divide by 8

result is 7/8 or .875.

2.3 LOSS OF NUMERICAL ACCURACY

2.3.1 A note on approximations

t is important to note that when we convert from a decimal fraction to a binary fraction, the result is, in general, an approximation expressed to a fixed number of bits, since, in general, the result is a recurring binary fraction.

The importance lies in the fact that we feed into the computer numbers expressed as decimals. These may be exact or they may already be approximations. The computer then converts them into binary, and the results of its conversions are usually approximations. All its arithmetic is then carried out upon these approximations (in binary). At the end of the calculations, the results are converted back to decimal before being printed out for human consumption.

Calculations on a computer using binary arithmetic and involving fractions usually will not produce exact answers in decimal. The best possible result is a close approximation. On the other hand, we *can* expect exact arithmetic when only *integers* are concerned.

2.3.2 Floating point format storage for approximations to real numbers

n general, two forms of internal representation of numbers occur inside a computer:

(i) Representation for integers only.

(ii) Representation for real numbers.

Note: If we are storing a *real* number whose value happens to be an integer, its value is still stored as a *real* number. If we are storing an *integer* its value will be stored as an *integer*.

Floating point representation uses two distinct values to represent a numbe:

　(i)　The mantissa.
　(ii)　The index (or exponent).

For example, in the denary notation, if we write:

　55791×10^{23},
　then the mantissa is 55791,
　the index is 23,
　and the base is 10 (denary).

For example, in the binary system, if we write:

　1111×10^{101},
　then the mantissa is 1111 (15 denary),
　the index is 101 (5 denary),
　and the base is 10 (2 denary),
　that is, (1111×10^{101}) binary
　(15×2^{5}) denary.

　　Inside the computer, both the mantissa and the index are commonly store‹
in 2's complement form, and the base is 2.

　　It should be appreciated that the binary pattern used to store an intege‹
will be totally different from the pattern used to store a real number having th‹
same (integer) value.

2.3.3　The effects of using approximations of finite length

Here is a highly revealing experiment you should carry out, either on a com‹
puter, or on a pocket calculator.

　　The object of the experiment may sound crazy, but it is not. The object i‹
to find the smallest number (let us call it epsilon) such that:

　$1 < 1 + \epsilon$
but
　$1 = 1 + \epsilon/2$.

The experiment is more revealing if carried out on a pocket calculator becaus‹
it is then easier to see what is happening, and why. To carry out the experimen‹
perform the following actions:

　Initial action:
　　Enter the value 1.

　Subsequent actions (to be repeated):
　　Divide by 2 and write down the result.
　　Add 1.
　　Subtract 1.

If the result is not zero,
repeat 'Subsequent actions',
otherwise go on to 'Final action'.

Final action:
Note the last result written down — this is the required value. Also count the number of results written down — this is the (inverse) power of 2 of which the last result is the value, epsilon.

.3.4 Distinguish between machine epsilon and minimum value which can be represented in the memory of a particular machine

lere is experiment number two (using the same computer, or the same pocket-alculator):

Initial action:
Enter the value epsilon.

Subsequent actions (to be repeated):
Divide by 2.
If the result is not zero, write it down,
and then repeat 'Subsequent actions',
otherwise go on to 'Final action'.

Final action:
Note the last result written down. This is the smallest value which can be stored in the computer (or pocket-calculator).

he value just found we shall call '*minreal*'.

.3.5 Machine accuracy

Ve have seen that calculations on a digital computer (or calculator), using fixed-ength representation of values, introduces the necessity of using approximations. Vhen using approximations, it is well to be aware that they are approximations nd not exact values, and to be aware that there is a certain degree of error resent.

The error of approximation, or accuracy of the result, depends partly upon he precision with which values are represented (that is, stored) inside the nachine. A measure of this accuracy is given by the values of ϵ and of *minreal* or any particular machine, because they represent limits, or contraints upon vhat can be achieved with that machine.

However, the way in which calculations are organised may introduce other rrors of approximation. The study of such effects belongs properly to the ubjects of numerical analysis and numerical methods, and will not be covered n this book, but it is essential for a programmer to be aware of their existence nd importance.

2.4 OCTAL AND HEXADECIMAL REPRESENTATION

Binary representation, even of positive integers, is very clumsy and inconvenien for human beings to read and write. There are two other number systems s closely related to binary that they provide, incidentally, convenient shorthand for binary. For this reason, they are widely used in descriptive computer litera ture, and whenever a binary coding is required. They are the octal (that is, eight based) and the hexadecimal (that is, sixteen-based) systems.

An integer value expressed in binary requires a relatively large number o bits. For example, the value 4095 (base ten) is 111111111111 in binary. Twelv bits are almost unreadable by a human. The readability may be greatly improve by grouping the bits into groups of three, or of four, for example:

    111, 111, 111, 111
or
    1111, 1111, 1111.

Both of these are very much easier to read. And we can go a step further. Th binary value 111 is equivalent to 7 (whether in octal or base ten). So it immediately clear that we may write 4095 (base 10) as 7777 (base eight, that i octal). In fact any group of three bits has a value which belongs to the se zero through seven, and hence may be expressed as an octal digit.

The hexadecimal number system is base-sixteen. It therefore require additional digit-numerals to represent the values 10, 11, 12, 13, 14 and 15 (bas ten) and for this purpose it is usual to use the letters A to F. The four-bit grou 1111 has the denary value 15, and the hexadecimal value F. Hence 4095 (bas ten) may be written, in binary 111111111111, in octal 7777, or in hex FFF.

2.5 BINARY CODING OF CHARACTERS

2.5.1 ASCII code

We have seen that numerical values may be represented in binary form, and tha this form is convenient for storage of information in electronic devices. It is clea that in order to store non-numeric information, it is convenient first to code i into numeric form and then to represent this as a binary number. This proces is known as binary coding. Table 2.3 shows part of the international 7-bit cod known as ASCII.

2.5.2 Use of shift characters

A complete set of different characters is called an 'alphabet'. Thus a 5-bit cod has an 'alphabet' of 32 characters. But this number may be effectively increase by the introduction of 'shift' characters. The 5-bit code commonly used b Creed teleprinters had two shift-codes, a 'letter shift' and a 'figure shift'. Eac of the remaining thirty codes was mapped to two characters, one belonging to the 'letter' set and the other to the 'figure' set. This scheme enabled a 5-bit code to have an alphabet of 60 different characters.

Note: A similar idea is used on typewriter keyboards, depression of any one key may print either of two possible characters (for example, upper-case or a lower-case letter), depending upon which 'shift' the carriage is in).

Table 2.3 – Part of the international 7-bit code known as ASCII.

Character	Binary code	Octal value	Hex
space	0 100 000	040	20
!	0 100 001	041	21
"	0 100 010	042	22
#	0 100 011	043	23
$	0 100 100	044	24
A	1 000 001	101	41
B	1 000 010	102	42
Y	1 011 001	131	59
Z	1 011 010	132	5A
0(zero)	0 110 000	060	30
1	0 110 001	061	31
8	0 111 000	070	38
9	0 111 001	071	39

2.5.3 Error detection

Transmission of binary-coded information is, of course, subject to 'noise', which causes errors. The great majority of code-words containing an error have only 1 bit wrong.

If the probability of 1 bit in a word being wrong is 1 in 1,000,000, then clearly the probability of a word containing two wrong bits is 1 in 1,000,000,000,000.

Single-bit errors are easy to detect if one extra check-bit is added to the information code being used. Such a bit is called a 'parity bit'. Its value is chosen as 0 or 1 in such a way as to maintain either odd or even parity throughout the code. If *even* parity is preserved, then every code word contains an *even* number of *ones*. If a check bit is added to the code words shown in Section 2.5.1 belonging to the ASCII, they become as shown in Table 2.4.

Table 2.4 – Code words belonging to ASCII with check bit added.

7-bit	8-bit including parity
0 100 000	10 100 000
0 100 001	00 100 001
0 100 010	00 100 010
0 100 011	10 100 011
0 100 100	00 100 100
1 000 001	01 000 001
1 000 010	01 000 010
1 011 001	01 011 001
1 011 010	01 011 010
0 110 000	00 110 000
0 110 001	10 110 001
0 111 000	10 111 000
0 111 001	00 111 001

2.5.4 Hexadecimal coding

When information is coded into 8-bit binary form, then by far the most convenient way of representing it for human purposes is as pairs of hex digits, each hex digit representing one group of four bits.

The standard word-length for mini-computers is 16 bits, micro-computers use 8-bit or 16-bit words, and very many large computers use 32-bit words. All of these word-lengths are multiples of 4 bits, and so hexadecimal representation is extremely convenient.

2.5.5 Mapping data from a large alphabet to a smaller one

Not all computers use the same size alphabet of characters for representation of data. Furthermore, nor do all data channels. The transmission of data therefore, sometimes has to cope with the problem of representing data which uses, say, a 256-character alphabet (for example, EBCDIC) in a smaller alphabet, say, a commonly available sub-set of ASCII, using at most 64 characters.

One way of solving such a problem is to introduce an extra level of coding, using hex. For example, 8-bit characters may be re-coded as a pair of hex digits. This process effectively maps a 256-character alphabet into a 16-character alphabet without any loss of information – the price paid of course being to double the number of characters, and to introduce the extra level of coding (and decoding at some later stage).

2.6 PROBLEMS

2.6.1

Subtract 010001 from 0110101 (both 2's complement binary) by finding the 2's complement of 010001 and adding it to 0110101. Check your result by transforming the two operands and the result into denary representation.

2.6.2

Convert the fractional binary number 01011.10101 to a decimal fraction.

2.6.3

Convert the negative decimal number -37.71 into binary.

2.6.4

The value of machine-epsilon for a particular computer is here represented by ϵ. If you wished to compute, numerically, the value of the derivative $D(x)$ of a given mathematical function:

$f(x)$ at the point $x = a$,

you could compute an approximation:

$$D(a) = (f(a + ah) - f(a))/ah$$

using a small value for h. Several Suggestions are made as to the value you should use:

(i) 0.01
(ii) 2ϵ
(iii) $\epsilon/2$.

Comment on the result you would expect, using each of these values. Which of the three would you recommend.

2.6.5

Write an algorithm for adding together two binary numbers (assuming that adding any two bits together produces a known pair of results, the sum and the carry, each of which is a bit, that is, 1 or 0).

CHAPTER 3

Very simple programs

$$\frac{\begin{array}{r}365\\1\end{array}}{364}$$

Humpty Dumpty took the book, and looked at it carefully. 'That seems to be right –' he began. 'You're holding it upside down!' Alice interrupted.

Lewis Carroll

3.1 ASSIGNMENT STATEMENTS

The concepts underlying assignment statements were discussed in Section 1.5. An assignment statement puts a value into a store location. Any value stored previously in that location is erased, overwritten by the new value, and lost. Before the initial (that is, the first) assignment of a value to a particular location, that location does not have any defined value. We say that the value of the variable whose identifier refers to that location is undefined.

$$x := 3$$

is an assignment statement, which we read as 'x takes the value 3'. The assignment operator consists of the two characters, 'colon' followed immediately by 'equals'.

A variable always occurs on the left of an assignment operator, and it refers to the location whose value (contents) is to be changed. If a variable occurs on the right of an assignment operator, it does not denote a location, but the contents of that location.

3.2 ARITHMETIC EXPRESSIONS

The expression on the right of an assignment statement may be an arithmetical expression. Quite complicated expressions are allowed in Pascal. There are two basic types of arithmetical value, *integer*, and *real*. We have already seen that the method of internal storage of *integers* is likely to differ from that of *real* numbers.

Similarly, in some respects, we must distinguish the arithmetical operations carried out on *reals* from those on *integers*. This distinction is not quite so important in the case of the operators add, subtract and multiply as it is for divide. But we do need to remember that *integer* arithmetic gives *exact* results whereas operations on *reals* yield only very accurate *approximations*.

The operators in Table 3.1 are defined for use with *integer* or *real* values even when mixed together.

Table 3.1

Operator symbol	Meaning
+	add
−	subtract
*	multiply
/	divide

The operators in Table 3.2 are defined *only* for use with *integer* type values.

Table 3.2

div	divide and truncate (that is, value is not rounded)
mod	$a \bmod b = a - (a \operatorname{div} b) * b$ (that is, the result yielded by $a \bmod b$ is the remainder on division of a by b).

EXAMPLES

(i) The expression $(k \bmod 2)$ yields the result 1 whenever k is odd, and zero whenever k is even.

(ii) The expression $(7 \operatorname{div} 2)$ yields the result 3.

The operator '/' denotes division as between *reals*. It may be used with *integers*, but always yields a *real* result.

EXAMPLE

$$3 \operatorname{div} 4 = 0$$

but

$$3/4 = 0.75$$

and

$$3.3/4.4 = 0.75$$

$3.3 \operatorname{div} 4.4$ is illegal (because it is undefined).

3.2.1 Precedence of operators

Arithmetic expressions may be built up as in mathematics, and the main rules for evaluation depend upon the precedence of operators, that is, the order in which different parts of the expression are evaluated. The order of precedence is as follows, highest precedence first:

```
(   )                brackets
*   /   div   mod    multiply and divide operators
+   −                plus and minus.
```

Those shown on the same line above have equal precedence.

EXAMPLE

$1.1 + 2.2*(3 - 0.5/2)$ gives the value 7.15.

Sometimes, the precedence rules are not sufficient to determine the order of evaluation, for example:

$6.0/2*3.0.$

The multiply and divide operators have equal precedence, so the result could be 9.0 or 1.0, depending on which operation is carried out first. This ambiguity is overcome by the left-to-right rule, which requires that evaluation be carried out from the left whenever operators have equal precedence.

3.3 STANDARD FUNCTIONS AND PROCEDURES

In addition to the standard arithmetic operators described, arithmetic expressions may make use of a number of common functions, which are provided as a standard feature of the Pascal language, including the following:

$abs(x)$ Computes the absolute value of x. The type of x must be either *real* or *integer*, and the type of the result is the type of x.
         (For $x > 0$, $abs(x) = x$
         for $x < 0$, $abs(x) = -x$
         $abs(0) = 0$).

$sqrt(x)$ Computes the square root of x, giving a *real* result.

$sin(x)$
$cos(x)$ Compute the trigonometric functions assuming the value of x to be in radians.
$arctan(x)$

$ln(x)$ Computes the natural logarithm of x.

$exp(x)$ Computes the exponential function of x.

For *sqrt, sin, cos, arctan, ln* and *exp*, the type of x must be either *integer* or *real*, and in all cases the result is of type *real*.

EXAMPLES OF VALID ARITHMETIC EXPRESSIONS USING STANDARD FUNCTIONS

   (i) $exp(4*ln(x) - 3*ln(y))$
   (ii) $sqrt(abs(4*a*c - b*b))$
   (iii) $sin(x)/cos(x)$

   Note: The trigonometric functions take the value of their parameter in radians.

EXAMPLES OF ASSIGNMENT STATEMENTS

$$x := x + 1$$
$$x := x + y$$
$$y := sqrt(u*u + v*v)$$
$$z := abs(z)$$
$$mean := 0.5*(a + b)$$
$$pi := 4*arctan(1)$$

3.4 SEQUENTIAL FILES – INPUT AND OUTPUT

3.4.1 Sequential files

A sequential file is merely a (logically complete) sequence of data-items (of similar type) stored on a sequential-acess memory device. This was introduced in Section 1.8, when data storage was discussed. It is useful to visualise a sequential file as a queue of data-items. When we *read* a sequential file, we are taking items from the head of the queue. When we *write* a sequential file, we are appending items to the tail of the queue.

In Pascal, the sequential file is defined as a structured type. All this means is that it is constructed from simpler types, such as *real, integer* (and others we shall introduce later). There are two most important sequential files which are standard files. That is to say we need not (and must not) declare them. They are 'pre-declared' for us by the Pascal system and their names are *input* and *output*.

The standard files *input* and *output* have certain special peculiarities not common to other sequential files:

(i) We are allowed to *read*, but not to *write* the file *input*.
(ii) We are allowed to *write*, but not to *read* the file *output*.

3.4.2 Input

When we wish to process data items stored in a sequential file, it is usually convenient to be able to refer to particular data items by name. To do this, it is necessary to *read* each item from the sequential file and store it in a (random-access) storage location denoted by an identifier, that is, a variable-name.

It is important to understand that the items of data in a sequential file appear to be queueing up to be read, so that an instruction in English such as:

'READ THE NEXT ITEM'

has a different meaning each time it is obeyed, because 'NEXT' refers to a new next each time the queue moves up.

When reading data from a sequential file, there is no need to specify 'the next item', since the only thing we can possibly read is the the next item; that is the essence of a sequential file. It is a file in which, at any particular moment, only the next item is accessible. However, it is necessary to specify the name of the variable to be used to store the item read. Hence the general form of the instruction for reading a single item, is:

read (filename, variablename)

where 'filename' must be replaced by the name of the file from which the data is to be read, and 'variablename' must be replaced by the name of the variable in which the data is to be stored. If the file to be read is the standard file *input*, then the filename may be omitted and only the variablename is required within the parentheses, for example:

read(*x*)

In addition to using the *read* instruction to read a single item, we may use it to read a sequence of items into a number of different variables, for example:

read(*U, V, W, X, Y, Z*)

will read the next six items from the file *input* and store them, in the order of reading, in the variables shown *U, V, W, X, Y, Z*. If several items of data are to be read, not from *input*, but from a different file, called *mydata*, then the appropriate instruction is, for example:

read(*mydata, a, b, c, d, e*)

It is important to understand that, although the form of the last two instructions is the same — each has six parameters following *read* — their meaning differs simply because *mydata* must have been declared in the program as a variable of type *file*, whereas the variables *a, b, ... e, U, V, ... Z*, have been declared as variables *not* of type *file*, but as say *integer* or *real*.

3.4.3 Output

The value (that is, contents) of a variable *x* may be written to the standard file '*output*' by means of the standard procedure '*write*', for example:

write(*x*)

To output the same information to a different file, called say *myfile*, the required instruction is:

write(*myfile, x*)

Just as with the case of *read*, *write* may be given a sequence of values to output, for example:

write(*u, v, w*)

will write the three values of *u, v, w*, in that order to the file *output*.

If we wish to output the value of an expression, this may be done directly, whether the expression is a constant or an expression involving variables, for example:

write(3.14159)
write(*x*∗*y* + 3)
write(*sqrt*(*x*∗*x* + *y*∗*y*))

The value to be output may also be a character-string. If so, it must be enclosed between quotation marks, for example:

write(' this is a character-string')

The output of character-strings together with values of variables can make the output of a program much more informative, for example:

write(' *x* = ',*x*, 'and *y* = ', *y*)

To move to the beginning of a new line of output, we use the instruction:

writeln

This may be given the same parameters as *write*, for example:

writeln(' *x* = ',*x*);
  write(' *y* = ',*y*)

The last two instructions will cause *two* separate lines of output, since a new line will be started immediately after the values output by *writeln*, and before execution of the *write* which follows.

3.5 THE STRUCTURE OF A PROGRAM

We have now introduced all the essential ingredients required for the construction of a simple program, namely:

  declarations of *real* and *integer* variables
  assignment instructions
  arithmetic expressions
  the standard functions
  the standard files *input* and *output*
  the standard procedures *read*, *write*, *writeln*.

An understanding of each of these ingredients and the ability to use each of them with confidence is vital before taking the next small, but crucial step of putting them together to make a program, and the equally crucial, complementary step of learning how to understand that program, how to interpret its meaning in an utterly definitive way.

We shall start by looking at programs whose meaning is so simple, that it does not distract our attention from their form, so simple that our immediate reaction is one of comprehension, not apprehension. Of course, no-one would ever bother to write such simple programs except for educational purposes. They are too trivial to be worth the effort of preparing and running on a computer. To do so is rather like using a hydraulic-press to crack an egg, and we shall call such programs 'silly' programs.

3.5.1 First example of a complete Pascal program

```
program silly1(input, output);
var x : real;
begin
  read(x);
  x := 2*x;
  write(x)
end.
```

There are a number of detailed features to note, as well as the all-important structural form of this program.

(i) Firstly, we distinguish three main parts of the program:
        program heading (line 1),
        declaration part (line 2),
        action part (lines 3 to 7).
(ii) These three parts are separated from each other by semi-colons (on lines 1 and 2).
(iii) The action part starts with the word **begin** and finishes with the word **end**. Between **begin** and **end**, there are three statements and these are separated from each other by (two) semi-colons (on lines 4 and 5).
(iv) The program heading starts with the word **program**, followed by an identifier which is the program-name, chosen by the writer of the program.
(v) After the program-name comes a list of identifiers; in this case two, separated by a comma. The list is enclosed in parentheses, and the identifiers denote the files used in this program. (The files used in this program are the standard files, *input* and *output*.)
(vi) The entire program is terminated by a full-stop.

Describing program structure in everyday English is very long-winded. One method of expressing this structure quite tersely and precisely is to use indentation as a means of indicating level of structure, for example:

program
  program heading
    program identifier (identifier-list)
  ;
  block
    variable-declaration-part
      var identifier-list : type
    ;
    statement-part
      begin statement-list **end**
  full-stop

There are a few elementary *do's* and *don'ts* to be noted:

don't   forget the full-stop at the end of a program,

do   make sure that program-heading, declarations, and statements are separated by semi-colons,

don't   make the mistake of thinking that every statement ends with a semi-colon, it doesn't.

3.5.2 Sample program 2

program *silly2* (*input, output*);
var *sum, x, y* : *real*;
begin
   read(x, y);
   sum := *sqrt*($x*x + y*y$);
   write(' square root of '
              , x, 'squared + '
              , y, 'squared = '
              , *sum*)
end.

It is perhaps worth pointing out that the *write* instruction in program *silly2* extends over 4 lines. A single statement does not have to be contained in a single line, and change to a new line in program generally has no significance. However, careful choice of where to start each new line in a program and the sensible use of identification and layout is of the highest importance in making the program easy to comprehend.

3.6 THE TRACE TABLE

We have dealt with the grammatical rules to be observed in a simple program but what of its meaning? The program is normally an attempt to define precisely and without ambiguity some algorithm which the programmer wishes the computer to execute. The meaning of a program is therefore what the computer does when it executes the program. This will vary slightly when different data values are supplied. However, we can test the meaning of a simple program quite effectively, by simulating what the computer does when the program is run with particular data which we supply.

We can simulate the actions of the computer, using pen and paper to do so, by constructing a table, line by line, which traces through the steps taken by the computer to execute the program. Each line of the table shows the step being executed, and indicates its effect in changing the values stored in the computer or recording values output by it.

3.6.1 Trace table for *silly* 1

Statement	*real x*	*output*
read(*x*) *x* := 2*∗x* *write*(*x*)	27.8 55.6	 55.6

input data for *silly*1: 27.8.

The headings of the columns of the trace table and the data list, correspond to the program heading and the declarations of the program.

The column headed *real x* corresponds to the variable *x*. The new contents of this location (that is, the value of *x*) at any point in time during the running of the program is given on the line corresponding to the end of execution of the program-step shown to the left of that line in the table.

3.6.2 Trace table for *silly* 2

Statement	Sum	*x*	*y*	*output*
read ... *sum* := ... *write* ...	 5.0	4.0	3.0	 4.0 squared + 3.0 squared = 5.0

input data for *silly*2: 4.0, 3.0.

Note: In a trace table, the current value of any variable is the value most recently written in its column. This value remains stored until it is changed by some subsequent statement in the program. Each change in value obliterates the previous value stored.

3.7 PROBLEMS

3.7.1

What is the value yielded by the following arithmetic expressions in a Pascal program?

  (i) $3.0/2.0*2.0$.
  (ii) $3.0/(2.0*2.0)$.
  (iii) $2.0 + 3.0*5.0$.
  (iv) $(2.0 + 3.0)*5.0$.
  (v) $6.0 - 2.0 + 1.0$.
  (vi) $6.0 - (2.0 + 1.0)$.
  (vii) $73 - 73\,\mathbf{div}\,8$.
  (viii) $7 - 7\,\mathbf{div}\,2$.
  (ix) $73\,\mathbf{mod}\,8$.
  (x) $73 - 8*(73\,\mathbf{div}\,8)$.

3.7.2

Which of the following assignment statements are illegal? For each legal statement, what value is assigned?

  (i) $x := sqrt(abs(5*5 - 4*4))$.
  (ii) $y := sqrt(abs(4*4 - 5*5))$.
  (iii) $u + v := 3$.
  (iv) $w := sqrt(sqrt(sqrt(16*81)))$.
  (v) $v := 8.3\,\mathbf{div}\,2.1$.

3.7.3

Construct a trace table for the program *silly2* using the *input* data: 8.0, 15.0.

3.7.4

Construct a trace table for the program *silly1* using the *input* data: −1.5.

CHAPTER 4

Logical operations

'Contrariwise,' continued Tweedledee, 'if it was so, it might be; and if it were
so, it would be: but as it isn't it ain't. That's logic.'

Lewis Carroll

4.1 BOOLEAN VARIABLES AND OPERATORS

In addition to variables of type *real*, that is, variables whose domain is the set
of *real* values, and variables of type *integer*, whose domain is the set of *integer*
values, we shall now introduce a new type of variable, called *boolean*, whose
domain consists of just two values, commonly denoted by '*true*', and '*false*', or
more briefly, by '1' and '0' respectively. Their inventor, the nineteenth-century
mathematician G. Boole developed an algebra in which these variables may
be manipulated, using a number of 'logical' operators. We shall describe the
behaviour of boolean variables under three of these operators, **and**, **or** and **not**
because the boolean expressions which may be constructed using these operators
are extremely useful tools in programming.

Just as the addition, and multiplication operators in arithmetic may be
defined quite simply and precisely by addition and multiplication tables, so
the boolean operators may be defined by tables called, 'truth tables'. In the
tables which follow (Tables 4.1 and 4.2), the letters P and Q are used as boolean
variables. These tables do not require justification or proof – they are definitions.

Table 4.1 – Truth table for NOT.

Q	Not$Q$
0	1
1	0

Table 4.2 – Combined truth table for AND and OR.

P	Q	P and Q	P or Q
0	0	0	0
0	1	0	1
1	0	0	1
1	1	1	1

The tables give exactly the same information as the following statements:

$$not\,1 = 0$$
$$not\,0 = 1$$
$$1\,and\,1 = 1$$
$$(1\,and\,0) = (0\,and\,1) = (0\,and\,0) = 0$$
$$(1\,or\,0) = (0\,or\,1) = (1\,or\,1) = 1$$
$$(0\,or\,0) = 0$$

Remember, '0' represents **false** and '1' represents **true**.

It is instructive to consider models in which the foregoing definitions have an obvious physical interpretation. Such a model is provided by simple electrical switching circuits, based upon the use of the electro-magnetic relay (Figs. 4.1 and 4.2). The relay is nothing more than a switch that is operated by a electro-magnet, consisting of a coil of wire with a laminated iron core (to increase the magnetic effect). When a current is passed through the coil, it operates the switch.

A switching circuit which behaves in the same way as a logical operator is known as a *logical gate*.

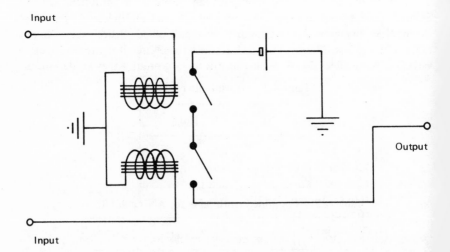

Fig. 4.1 – The **and** logical gate.

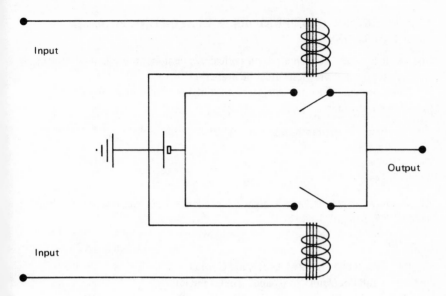

Fig. 4.2 — The **or** logical gate.

4.2 RELATIONAL OPERATORS

A simple form of boolean expression is a boolean variable, but it is easy to construct expressions which yield a boolean value by using numerical values together with relational operators. The relational operators in common use are:

$$<, \leqslant, =, \geqslant, >, \neq$$

some examples of boolean expressions follow:

Expression	Value
$4 = 5$	false
$3 = 3$	true
$8 = 9 - 3$	false
$(14 > 1)$ **or** $(3 = 0)$	true
$(14 > 1)$ **and** $(3 = 0)$	false
not $(14 > 1)$ **or not** $(3 = 0)$	true
not $((14 > 1)$ **and** $(3 = 0))$	true

A boolean expression may be assigned to any boolean variable which has been declared. A boolean variable must be declared, as follows:

var p : *boolean*

after which an assignment statement might be written, for example:

$p :=$ **not** $((14 > 1)$ **and** $(3 = 0))$

4.3 PRECEDENCE OF OPERATORS IN EVALUATING BOOLEAN EXPRESSIONS

Just as in the case of evaluating numerical expressions, there is a correct order in which boolean expressions must be evaluated.

The following list gives operators with highest order of preference first, and there is a strict order:

first	parentheses	( )
then	**not**	
next	**and**	
last	**or**	

All the above symbols have a higher precedence than the relational operators '=', '>', '<', etc.

EXAMPLES

A or B and C or $D = A$ or $(B$ and $C)$ or D

X and Y or U and $V = (X$ and $Y)$ or $(U$ and $V)$

P and not Q or not P and $Q = (P$ and $(\text{not} Q))$ or $((\text{not} P)$ and $Q)$

Note that:

$x > 3$ and $y < 6$

is nonsense, because the operator '**and**' takes precedence over the relational operators '>' and '<'. The meaning probably intended is conveyed by

$(x > 3)$ and $(y < 6)$

4.4 DE MORGAN'S LAW(S)

We may wish to *multiply out* an expression such as:

not $(X$ and $Y)$

that is, to obtain an equivalent expression with no brackets. It may come as a surprise to find that

not $(X$ and $Y) = $ not X or not Y

and this is easily verified by constructing the truth table for each expression; this exercise is recommended.

By means of truth tables, it is easy to verify the truth of De Morgan's two laws, which are:

(i) not $(X$ and $Y) = $ not X or not Y

(ii) not $(P$ or $Q) = $ not P and not Q

There is really only one law, with two equivalent alternative forms. To prove this, make the substitutions $P = \text{not}X$, $Q = \text{not}Y$ on left-hand side of (ii). The expression inside the brackets then becomes identical to the right-hand side of (i). The reader is left to complete the proof.

Mastery of De Morgan's laws is indispensable for ease of manipulation of boolean expressions, and the importance of this arises in the construction of conditional statements in the course of writing programs, particularly when conditional expressions of some complexity are required.

4.5 CONDITIONAL STATEMENTS

Most frequently, we need to determine, at some point in a program, which of two alternative statements should be executed. This requirement is met by using a conditional expression.

4.5.1 Examples
EXAMPLE (i)

```
if A > B
then write (' A greater')
else write (' A not greater')
```

EXAMPLE (ii)

```
if (X div 2)*2 = X
then write (' X is even')
else write (' X is odd')
```

EXAMPLE (iii)

```
program to solve a quadratic equation of form
a*x*x + b*x + c = 0
```

```
program quad (input, output);
var a, b, c, discriminant, twoa,
    term1, term2 : real;
    complex : boolean;
begin
  read (a,b,c);
  writeln (' quadratic with coefficients');
  writeln (a,b,c);
  discriminant := b*b — 4*a*c;
  twoa       := 2*a;
  term1      := —b/twoa;
  term2      := sqrt (abs (discriminant))/twoa;
  complex    := discriminant < 0;
```

```
if complex
then
   begin
      writeln(' complexroots');
      writeln(' real part = ', term1,
                  ' imag part = ', term2)
   end
else
   begin
      writeln(' real roots');
      writeln(' root 1 = ', term1 + term2,
                  ' root 2 = ', term1 − term2)
   end
end.
```

EXAMPLE (iv)

The following program reads in three arithmetic values and prints out the middle
value (assuming no two values are equal). It also uses the facility for inserting a
'comment' by inserting it between the curly brackets '{' and '}'. The inclusion
of comments has no effect upon the meaning of the program, but makes them
easier to comprehend.

```
program middle1(input, output);
var a, b, c : real;
begin
   read(a, b, c);
   writeln(a, b, c);
      if a > b
      then
         if b > c
         then writeln(b)
         else {b is smallest}
            if a > c
            then writeln(c)
            else writeln(a)
      else
         if a > c
         then writeln(a)
         else {a is smallest}
            if b > c
            then writeln(c)
            else writeln(b)
end.
```

EXAMPLE (v)
This program does the same as *middle*1, but uses a slightly different method.

```
program middle2(input, output);
var a, b, c, large, middle, small : real;
begin
  read(a, b, c);
  writeln(a, b, c);
    if a > b
    then
        begin
          large := a;
          small := b
        end
    else
        begin
          small := a;
          large := b
        end;
    if c > large
    then middle := large
    else
        if c < small
        then middle := small
        else middle := c;
  writeln(middle)
end.
```

4.5.2 Compound statements
The conditional statements occurring in the foregoing examples all have the form:

> if   BOOLEAN-EXPRESSION
> then STATEMENT-1
> else STATEMENT-2

In this form of conditional statement, each STATEMENT stands for a single statement. However, in examples (iii) and (vi) of Section 4.5.1, we needed a group of statements. When this happened, we turned the group of statements into a single statement which was a compound statement. This has the form:

```
begin
   STATEMENT-A;
   STATEMENT-B;
      •
      •
      •
   STATEMENT-K
end
```

We see that **begin** and **end** are used a parentheses to bracket together a sequence of statements and unify them into a single compound statement.

4.5.3 Conditional statement with no alternative

We have seen the conditional statement whose form is:

if   BOOLEAN-EXPRESSION
then STATEMENT-1
else STATEMENT-2

Sometimes we want STATEMENT-2 to be equivalent to 'DO NOTHING AT ALL'; and in such a case, the **else** part (and its STATEMENT-2) may be omitted altogether, thus:

STATEMENT-BEFORE-CONDITIONAL-STATEMENT;
if BOOLEAN-EXPRESSION
then STATEMENT-1;
STATEMENT-FOLLOWING-CONDITIONAL-STATEMENT

EXAMPLE:

if $x < 0$
then $x := -x$

4.6 PROBLEMS
4.6.1

Simplify the boolean expression by using De Morgan's laws:

p and not $(p$ or $q)$ or $(p$ or not $(p$ and $q))$

Check your solution by constructing a truth table for it and for the original expression.

4.6.2

Construct two trace tables for the program *quad* given in example (iii) of Section 4.5.1, using as *input* data:

(a) 1.0,   3.0,   2.0
(b) 1.0,   3.0,   6.25.

4.6.3

Construct three trace tables for each of the two programs *middle*1, *middle*2, given as examples (iv) and (v) in Section 4.5.1, using for each program as *input* data:

(a) 1.0,   2.0,   3.0
(b) 2.0,   1.0,   3.0
(c) 3.0,   1.0,   2.0.

4.6.4

Write a Pascal program which will read in any five arithmetic values, print them out in the order in which they were read in, and then print them out again in reverse order.

Construct a trace table for your program, using as *input* data:

10,   20,   30,   40,   50.

4.6.5

Construct truth tables to verify De Morgan's law, in both forms.

CHAPTER 5

Building-bricks of programming

'How is bread made?' 'I know that!' Alice cried eagerly. 'You take some flour —' 'Where do you pick the flower?' the White Queen asked. 'In a garden, or in the hedges?' 'Well it isn't picked at all,' Alice explained: 'It's ground —' 'How many acres of ground?' said the White Queen. 'You musn't leave out so many things.'

Lewis Carroll

5.1 LOOPS

Let us suppose that we used a program which reads and prints out the values of a sequence of positive integers provided as data. If the data consisted of just three values, then the following program will do:

```
program printdata(input, output);
var a, b, c : integer;
begin
  read(a, b, c);
  writeln(a, b, c)
end.
```

This program works correctly, but it is a bad program. Why is it a bad program? Think about this and try modifying it (while retaining its main form) to make it work when:

(i) The data consists of a sequence of 10 integers.
(ii) The data consists of a sequence of 1000 integers.

Clearly, the modification required for (ii) makes the program inordinately long. Furthermore, such a program has to be modified whenever the data contains a different number of values. To deal with this situation adequately we need a way of saying, in a program, 'do this part over and over again'. The programming structure which provides such a facility is called a *loop*. All loops have two basic characteristics. The first is repetition: the second is modification. Repetition means repeated execution of the instruction or sequence of instructions which form the *body* of the loop. Modification means that what is repeated is not exactly the same, although it looks the same. We met this idea before, in Section 3.4.2, where we saw that an instruction in English like

'read the next item'

has a different meaning each time it is obeyed, since *next* refers to new *next* each time it is invoked. Now, although all loops have these properties, there are several ways of writing them, which we shall look at one by one. The first is the **repeat** statement, and we use it to rewrite the program *printdata* as follows in the next section.

5.1.1 The repeat statement

```
program egrepeat(input, output);
var times, k : integer;
begin
  read(times);
  writeln(times);
  repeat
    read(k);
    writeln(k);
    times := times −1
  until times = 0
end.
```

This program is a wonderful improvement over *printdata* since it will deal with any number of data values, provided that number appears as the first data value, before all the others. This first value is read into the variable called *times*. We called it that because its value is the number of times the loop is to be repeated. The program ensures this by subtracting 1 from *times* within the body of the loop, that is, between **repeat** and **until**. The sequence of three instructions which constitute the body of the loop is executed repeatedly until the value of *times* is equal to zero. Thus if the data starts with the value 1000, the program will expect a thousand values to follow. If it starts with the value 29, then twenty-nine values will be expected to follow.

If the data list consists of the values:

    3,   57,   −2,   24

then the trace table for the program *egrepeat* is as shown in Table 5.1.

One interesting point about the repeat loop in *egrepeat* is that, at the time of writing the program, it is not known how many times the loop will be repeated, but this is known as soon as the first data value is determined. However, some loops are terminated not by counting at all, but by testing a calculated condition at each repetition.

There is a standard identifier, *maxint*, which does not have to be declared. It is a constant whose value is the greatest positive integer which can be stored in an *integer* type variable. Of course, it is likely to have different values on different computers, and is said to be a machine-dependent value.

Table 5.1 – Trace table for the program *egrepeat* using the data list consisting of the values 3, 57, −2, 24.

Statement or operation	boolean *times* = 0	integer *k*	integer *times*	output
begin				
read(*times*)			3	
read(*k*)		57		
write(*k*)				57
times := *times* − 1			2	
until test?	*false*			
read(*k*)		−2		
write(*k*)				−2
times := *times* − 1		1	1	
until test?	*false*			
read(*k*)		24		
write(*k*)				24
times := *times* − 1			0	
until test?	*true*			
end				

Suppose you want a program which will find the value of the highest power of two which can be stored on *any* machine on which the program is run. The following program will do just that.

```
program, maxpowerof2(output);
var halfmax, n, power : integer;
begin
    halfmax := maxint div 2;
    n := 1;
    power := 0;
    repeat
        n := n*2;
        power := power + 1;
    until n > halfmax;
        writeln(' maxint = ', maxint,
                ', power = ', power,
                ', n = ', n)
end.
```

It is worth noting that the body of the loop in a **repeat** statement is alway execute at least once. This is because the body of the loop is executed *befor* the boolean expression following **until** is tested.

It may happen that this is undesirable. We may wish to test our loop-ex condition before executing the body of the loop, so that in some circumstance the loop-body is not executed at all. This kind of loop is provided by the **whi** statement.

5.1.2 The while statement

Suppose we require a program which reads in an integer value and prints ou the value of its largest odd factor (that is, the value left after performing a many exact divisions by two as are possible). Then the following program *maxoddfactor* will do this.

```
program maxoddfactor(input, output);
var k : integer;
begin
  read(k);
  write(' highest odd factor of', k, 'is');
    while k mod 2 = 0
    do k := k div 2;
  writeln(k)
end.
```

If the data value read into this program is an odd number, then the boolea expression following **while** will evaluate to *false*, and hence the loop body wi be executed zero times. If, however, the data value read in is say 52, then th boolean expression will be found to be true both the first and second times is evaluated, hence the loop will be executed twice, reducing the value of k fro 52, first to 26 and then to 13. The third time the boolean expression is evaluate it will be *false*, because $13 \bmod 2 = 1$, so the loop is immediately terminated an execution proceeds to the statement immediately following the **while** statemen

5.1.3 The for statement

The third kind of loop structure provided in Pascal is useful when it is known a the time of writing the loop that counting is involved in two distinct ways:

  (i) in counting the number of repetitions of the loop,
     or
  (ii) the current value of the count is itself used in some way in the calc lation contained in the loop body.

For example, consider the following program, which calculates the sum of th first n terms of the series:

$$1 + 1/2 + 1/3 + \ldots + 1/n$$

```
program egfor(input, output);
var k, n : integer;
    sum : real;
begin
  sum := 0;
  read(n);
    for k := 1 to n
    do sum := sum + 1/k;
    writeln(' for n = 1 to ', n, ', sigma 1/n = ', sum)
end.
```

n a **for** loop such as the one in *egfor*, the variable k is known as the loop control ariable; and the *initial value* and *final value* in this example are expressions 1 nd n, respectively. In a **for** loop, the control variable, and initial and final values ust all be of same type, and they are not allowed to be *reals*, because you annot *count* with *reals*.

Sometimes it is convenient to use the alternative form of **for** statement. his would replace the line beginning with **for** in the *egfor* program by

for $k := n$ **downto** 1

eaving the remainder of the program unchanged. The sense of the two versions identical, but the order of evaluation of the terms in the series is reversed. For large value of n, the order of evaluation of terms could affect the accuracy of he calculation, so the two versions of this program might give slightly different esults (see Section 2.3).

The three forms of loop statement we have seen, are characterised then as ollows:

   (i) **repeat** statement
        loop-exit condition tested *after* loop-body;
        loop-body executed at least *once*.
  (ii) **while** statement
        loop-exit condition tested *before* loop-body;
        loop-body executed zero or more times.
(iii) **for** statement
        useful when the loop-body makes explicit use of the repetition
        count (that is, of the number of times the loop-body has currently
        been executed);
        control variable must not be of type *real*;
        the expressions for initial and final values are calculated once only.

Of course, it is possible to force any required loop into an unsuitable form. hoice of the most suitable form is good programming style which improves the larity and readability of the program. This is most important, not only for the enefit of readers of the program, but because to seek clear expression of neaning is an aid to clarity of thought.

5.2 COMPOUND STATEMENTS

A compound statement is nothing more than a sequence of statements which are bracketed together and thereby unified into a single, compound statement. This is an invaluable device, commonly used in the construction of a loop, in order to make the body of the loop include several statements. In the **repeat** statement form of the loop, the delimiters, **repeat** and **until** act as the brackets. (*Note*: All the words printed in bold-face type in Pascal programs are called delimiters.) In both the **while** and the **for** statement forms of loop, the body of the loop is the single statement following the delimiter **do**. If more than one statement is required in the loop body following **do** then several statements are bracketed together by using the delimiters **begin** and **end**.

    The **begin** and **end** brackets are used in the same kind of way in conditional statements, to bracket together into a single compound statement several statements following **then**, or following **else** (see Section 4.5.2).

5.3 FLOW CHARTS

A flow chart is a pictorial means of illustrating the flow of control through a program when it is executed. The arrow markings on the lines indicate the permitted direction of flow of control, and the boxes are of three fundamental shapes:

    (i) THE CIRCLE. This is reserved for points of entry to or exit from the chart.

    (ii) THE DIAMOND. This is a decision or branch point. A diamond shaped box has one entry line and two possible exit lines, one marked *true* and the other *false*. The exit line to be taken is determined by the value of the boolean expression written inside the box.

    (iii) THE RECTANGLE. This is an action box. It can have exactly one exit line. Its contents may be a single statement, a group of statements or a whole block of program represented elsewhere by its own flow chart.

5.3.1 The repeat loop flow chart

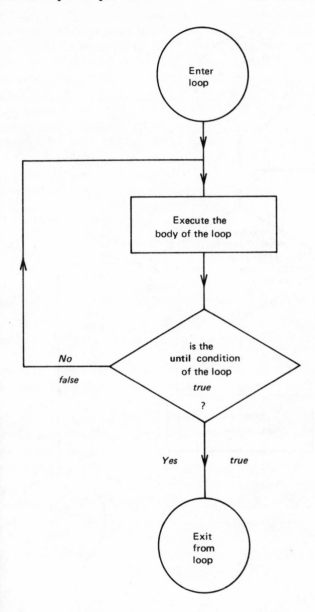

5.3.2 The while loop flow chart

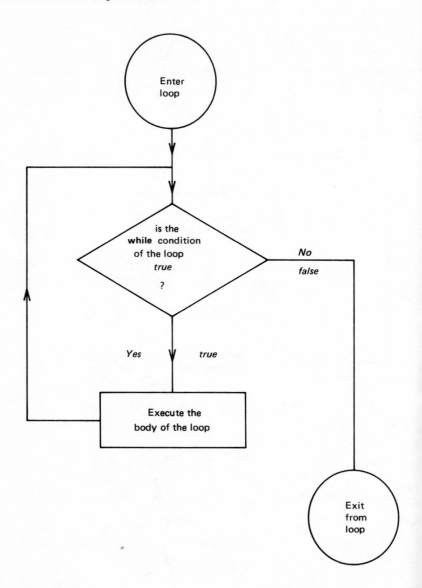

3.3 The for loop flow chart

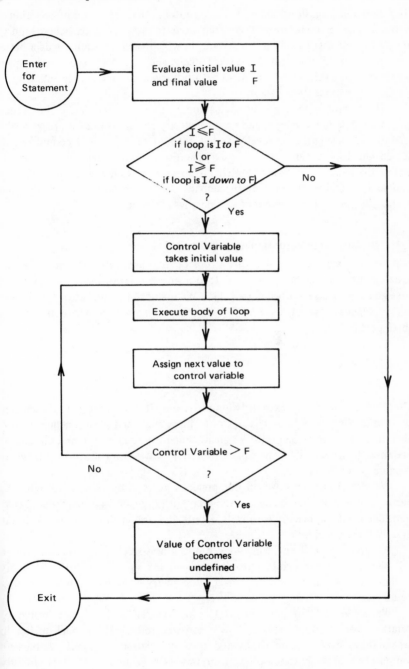

5.4 ITERATION

The common English meaning of the word iteration is repetition of an action or process; and in computing it is often used to describe a particular kind of repetitive process, usually a calculation, in which each iteration yields a better approximation to the desired answer. Usually, such a process starts with a guess at the answer; this guess may be quite arbitrary, and some simple rule may be devised for making such a guess.

The improvement made at each iteration may be small, but if the process of iteration is fairly simple, and easy to specify in the form of a program, this method of calculating is ideally suited to modern high-speed computers, on which the time taken for the basic operations of arithmetic is measured in millionths of a second. Some iterative processes improve the result quite quickly and so are suitable for use even by humans. A classic example of such a process is that for finding the square root of a positive real number.

5.4.1 Iterative method for finding a square root

Suppose we wish to find the square root of the quantity a. We know that the square root of a lies between a and 1, so a simple rule for making an arbitrary first guess is to take the value $(a + 1)/2$. We shall call this first guess x. Consider what happens if we divide a by x and obtain the result y. There are exactly three possibilities:

(i) $y = x$
(ii) $y > x$
(iii) $y < x$.

The first possibility is extremely unlikely, but, if true, then x is the desired result and there is nothing left to do. If, however, x and y are unequal factors of a, then the greater one must be greater than the square root, and the smaller one must be smaller than the square root. The square root must lie somewhere in value between x and y.

We can clearly improve on our previous guess x, by replacing it with the mean of x and y, that is, by the value $(x + y)/2$, giving us a new value, say z. Consider what happens if we divide a by z and obtain the result w. There are exactly three possibilities...

We are now well and truly locked into a non-stop merry-go-round which will give us ever-improving approximations to the square root of a. The only remaining problem is how to get off the merry-go-round — when to stop iterating.

We could test for possibility (i) before starting on each new round of iteration, for example, does $z = w$? However, since real numbers do not in general have *exact* square roots, and since calculation with *real* numbers on computers is not an exact process anyway (see Section 2.3), it is virtually impossible for the $z = w$ situation to occur. Moreover, we are seeking an approximate value, not an exact value of the square root, so a more sensible test is to measure the error of our latest approximation, that is, the ratio of the difference and sum of z and w. If we are satisfied with a result which is within one per cent of the right answer them we can stop iterating when, taking the absolute (numerical) values of z and w, regardless of sign, we find that

$$(z - w)/(z + w) < 0.01$$

We shall now consider how to go about writing a program (using this algorithm) to calculate the square root of a real positive number.

5.5 HOW TO WRITE A SIMPLE PROGRAM

Rule 1 is:
Don't start *writing* — start *thinking*.

There is a lot of thinking to do before writing a program, and not very much thinking to do while writing it. If you find this is not true, put down your pen and go back to rule 1. The thinking before writing can be divided into stages:

- (i) Has the problem been specified without ambiguity, and with sufficient information?
- (ii) Have you a simple algorithm for solving the problem?
- (iii) Can you simplify the algorithm?
- (iv) What is the central process which lies at the heart of the algorithm?

Rule 2 is:
Don't *write* your program — *construct* it.

For the program we are about to construct, the preliminary thinking was described in Section 5.4.1, but a little more thinking is always a good thing (iteration on rule 1). The quantities we discussed in Section 5.4.1 seemed to keep changing their names, first x and y, then y and z, then z and w, ... though their relative *roles* stayed the same. For each iteration, we are concerned with the following quantities:

> The number whose square root is required.
> The current or old estimate of the square root.
> The new estimate of the square root.
> The relative error at this stage.
> The maximum relative error to be permitted in final result.

It is always useful to choose short but meaningful names for the quantities with which one is calculating, and to use these names as identifiers in the program. A possible choice for the five just listed, in the same order, is:

> *a, old, new, relerr, max.*

Now we are ready to start constructing our program.

> The place to start is in the middle.

This is logical and important. Our thinking takes us straight to the heart of the program, to the process at the heart of each iteration, and we should now be ready to write it down and look at it:

$$new := (a/old + old)/2$$

This is simply a translation into Pascal from the process previously thought out in English, as:

> divide a by the old guess, and the new guess is the mean of the old guess and the result of the division.

It is of course, more concise, more precise, and actually easier to read in Pascal than it is in English. But then Pascal was designed for this sort of thing. Let us continue with program construction. We already know that we wish to repeat the process which calculates *new* until *relerr* is less than *max*:

repeat
    $new := (a/old + old)/2$

until *relerr* $<$ *max*

Notice there are several blank lines between the one starting '*new* . . .' and the one starting '**until**', because, *before* writing, we knew that:

(i) we actually have to calculate the value of *relerr* inside the body of the loop, as soon as we have calculated *new* from *old*,
(ii) before going on to the next iteration we must 'change the name' of the quantity represented by *new*, ready for its 'new' role as *old*.

repeat
    $new := (a/old + old)/2$
    $relerr := abs(new - old)/(new + old);$
    $old := new$
until *relerr* $<$ *max*

That completes the construction of our basic iteration loop. The next thing to do is to consider what quantities need to be given initial values before entering the **repeat** loop. These are *a*, *max*, and *old*. It makes sense to read in the values of *a* and *max*, and we already know how to make a first guess at *old*, so immediately before the loop, we want the statements:

read (*a*, *max*);
old := (*a* + 1)/2;

That seems to take care of the calculation part of the program. After exit from the loop, we shall want to print some information. The result alone is not very informative. It is essential to put it in context by descriptive comment, and to relate the result to the data from which it was produced. Something like:

write (' square root of', *a*, 'subject to relative error');
writeln (*max*, ' = ', *new*)

All that remains is to put in the program heading and declaration part. We are now ready to write the program.

5.5.1 Program to find the square root of a real positive number to an accuracy within a specified relative error

```
program squareroot (input, output);
var a, old, new, relerr, max : real;
begin
    read (a, max);
    {program to find square root of a, with maximum relative error max}
    old := (a + 1)/2;
        repeat
            new := (a/old + old)/2;
            relerr := abs (new − old)/(new + old);
            old := new
        until relerr < max;
            write (' square root of', a,
                    'within relative error of',
                    max);
            writeln (' = ', new)
end.
```

5.6 THE COMPUTING PROCESS AND ERROR REPORTS

In his monumental, seven-volume work, 'The Art of Computer Programming', Donald Knuth writes that preparing programs for a computer 'can be an aesthetic experience much like composing poetry or music'. This is quite true, but programming encompasses more than being an art, it is also a technology. We ask first of a program, 'Does it work?', and only then are we ready to consider its beauty, its elegance, its poetry. In an *idealised* world, every program is constructed in parallel with a mathematical proof of its correctness; in this way, the writing of incorrect programs is avoided. In the more familiar world of everyday experience, it may be found more difficult to construct the mathematical proofs than the programs themselves. The fact is that the number of computer programs written, even by professionals, which are correct, amounts to a very small proportion of the programs they write.

When we wish to answer the important question 'does this program work?' we know the odds are that it doesn't, and we devise test procedures which try to demonstrate that it doesn't. Well-designed testing puts a program through its paces over a range of the typical conditions in which it might run. It is usually either impossible or impracticable to test *all possible* conditions. Even though a program survives well-designed tests, it is not thereby proved correct, but for practical purposes it is acceptable.

The most practical and obvious way of testing a program is to run it, on a real computing system. Such a system appears superficially to be very different from the abstract model described in Section 1.9, and running a program may entail learning to prepare punched cards or to use a keyboard terminal or teletype, to 'log in' to a computer, to learn an arbitrary process required for communication with a particular machine, which requires the rigid observance of innumerable petty rules. The frustration suffered by many first-time computer users can be very far indeed from an aesthetic experience. If you have ever tried to start a cold and stubborn car-engine, with a nearly flat battery, in a dark country lane, having just changed a wheel in the rain after a puncture, you will know all about the poetic joys of motoring in the countryside. The real poetry comes from man's mastery over the machine, and this is won by learning not just how it works, but also how the nuts and bolts fit together.

When a Pascal program is submitted to a computer, there are usually two main stages in the computing process. The first stage is one of translation of the program from Pascal into a code which can be interpreted as machine-orders by the computer. This stage is called *compilation*. The Pascal program is called the *source* program, and the code compiled from it is called the *object-code*. The large and complex computer program which carries out this compilation is called a Pascal compiler. The compiler processes its *data*, that is, the Pascal source program, by checking it for correct syntax, to ensure that it is indeed a valid Pascal program, amenable to compilation (that is, translation). If errors, for example, syntax errors, are detected at compile-time, the compiler will issue diagnostic messages intended to help the programmer correct the errors. These error-messages are sometimes rather cryptic, but they usually provide enough information to be helpful, if only we study them carefully. If there are serious errors detected at compile-time, then no object-code program is produced. However, if the compilation-time checking is successful, then a complete machine-code program is produced, ready to *run* or *execute* in the second main stage of the computing process, known as run-time, or execution-time.

.6.1 The operating system

'he computing system itself is managed and supervised by a program much arger and more complex than a compiler, called an operating system. The perating system reads and interprets job control commands, arranges to make vailable to each job the compiler it requires, organises the two phases of the job, nd takes action to end the job prematurely in the event of any programming rrors occurring which it has been programmed to treat as catastrophic.

Thus some run-time errors are detected by the operating system, others by he run-time programs which form part of the Pascal compiler. Some typical un-time errors are now described.

.6.2 Run-time errors. Case study 1 – time limit exceeded

A program may exceed the time limit set for it by the operating system. This nay happen as a result of sharply differing causes which call for quite different emedial action. The computer will tell you that the time limit has been xceeded, but it will not tell you why. That is something you have to learn to liscover for yourself.

```
program endlessloop(input, output);
var n : integer;
    sum : real;
{program to sum the first n terms of the series 1 + 1/2 + ... + 1/n}
begin
    sum := 0;
    read(n);
      repeat
        sum := sum + 1/n;
        n := n - 1
      until n = 0;
    writeln(' for', n, 'terms, sum = ', sum)
end.
```

Imagine that you run the above program, using as data a value of n less han 50, and, surprise, surprise, you get no output apart from an error message aying 'time limit exceeded'. Since the amount of computation involved is rivial, you know it cannot be that the program needs more time than the limit llowed, and you smile condescendingly at those fellow students who advise you to run it again, asking for more time. No, it is clear that somehow, the program has got itself into a never-ending loop. But how? You look at the program again, and check its logic, but find nothing wrong. Being conscientious, you remember that a better way of checking the logic is to construct a trace able, and you proceed to do so, using the data value for n of say, 3. The program still appears to work correctly. You sit and fume for a while, experiencing the aesthetic joy of running through your entire vocabulary of denigratory epithets and applying them to the computer, the program, all computers, all programs, etc. This increases the adrenalin to a level sufficient to overcome your natural shyness, and you take your program and computer output to the local expert and demand an explanation.

The explanation is quite simple, but is actually not very important. What is important is to learn how to modify this program, and how to write other programs in such a way as to *minimise your frustration*. Minimisation of frustration requires a certain kind of programming style, one which makes errors more obvious, one which gives *maximum information* when errors occur.

From the point of view of minimisation of frustration, the most important modification to the program *endlessloop* is to insert, immediately following the instruction, '*read*(*n*)', an instruction, '*writeln*(*n*)'. This should ensure that the computer output for the program will show clearly the value of the data which caused the run to terminate with the error-message 'time exceeded'. (You just may have guessed by now that the explanation is simply that you accidentally and unintentionally input a negative value of *n*).

A second criticism of the program *endlessloop* is that you did not choose the most suitable loop structure. The program would be clearer, simpler, and less subject to error if the loop were rewritten, using an *integer* control variable *k* (which must be declared), as follows:

> **for** $k := n$ **downto** 1 **do**
> $sum := sum + 1/k;$

Of course, having modified your program in the two respects described, you might still accidentally input a negative data value, but the computer output would then give sufficient information for you to see what had gone wrong much more quickly, with much less frustration, and without wasting time.

5.6.3 Run-time errors. Case study 2 — time limit exceeded

A user has the following problem. There is a well-defined but complicated mathematical function $f(p, q, r)$ whose value for any given set of values of p, q, and r takes about one minute of computer time to calculate. The parameters p, q and r can each take each of the integer values from 1 to 50. Our user wishes to calculate the average of all the possible values of f, and has written a program to do this.

```
program meanf(input, output);
var mean, f, sum : real;
    a, b, c, p, q, r : integer;
begin
  p := 50;
  q := 50;
  r := 50;
```

```
sum := 0;
    for a := 1 to p do
    for b := 1 to q do
    for c := 1 to r do
    begin
        {calculate current value of f}
        •
        •
        •
        sum := sum + f
    end;
    mean := sum/(p*q*r);
    writeln(' mean =', mean)
end.
```

He has run the program several times, each time getting no output except for the error-message 'time-limit exceeded'. On the following run he has used an increased value of time limit; but his last run used the maximum time limit allowed at the computer centre, so he does not know what to do.

What he should do is to find a different problem. If a calculation of f takes one minute, then $50 \times 50 \times 50$ minutes is the time required for his program, that is, 125,000 minutes. This works out to be something over 86 days (24 hours a day) of continuous computer time. Sometimes an innocuous looking program turns out to demand an enormous amount of time, especially if it contains loops within loops within loops.

If you have a problem which requires loops like that, do the necessary arithmetic first, without a computer. It can save you and the computer lots of time.

5.6.4 Run-time errors of arithmetic

It is easy to generate very large numbers in some calculations, especially scientific calculations. (For example, Avogadro's constant, the number of molecules in a gram of Hydrogen, is approximately 3.10×10^{23}.) There are many ways in which, in the course of execution of a program, numbers may be generated which are too large for the computer to store (within the standard space it usually provides for *real* numbers). An obvious example is division by zero, but the same effect follows upon division of a large number by a very small one. The program may include a division in which the divisor is the difference between two variables. If this difference becomes very small then we get the same problem. We therefore are obliged to approach the programming of calculations with great care, and to be on the lookout for trouble, and for ways to avoid it. One way of avoiding numbers which are too large (or too small) is to compute critical parts of the calculation in terms of logarithms. The cost of this is in both computer time and in precision of the result.

Another kind of arithmetical run-time error arises from trying to compute some function, for example, one of the standard functions such as *ln* or *sqrt*, using a parameter whose value (at the time of calculation) is outside the domain of values of parameter for which the function is defined. This error occurs if the *ln* or the *sqrt* is taken of a variable whose current value is negative.

5.6.5 Not enough data values

Not enough data values to satisfy the expectations of the *read* instructions in the program may be either a programming error, or it may be an error in preparation of the data. The message given by different computers to indicate this error is not always clear. Some examples are:

> end of file
> unchecked end of file
> input ended
> data exhausted
> no data
> attempt to read beyond end of information
> end of data encountered before end of program

Usually, the data to be supplied to a program fits into some kind of structured pattern, and it helps to avoid the error under discussion if this pattern is made obvious, both in the program itself, and in the data. For example, if the data for program *egrepeat* in Section 5.1.1 were on cards, it would make sense to have the first card containing only one value, the value read into *times*, and the remaining cards containing a regular constant number of values on each card. This makes it easy to check the number of values in the data. If the data for a program consists of sets of, say, three values, and there is a number of such sets, then it is sensible to prepare the data cards with three values per card.

5.7 PROBLEMS

5.7.1

Write a Pascal program to find the (machine-dependent) quantity *epsilon*, using the algorithm described in Section 2.3.3, and then write a second program, using the algorithm described in Section 2.3.4 to find the quantity *minreal*.

5.7.2

Write a Pascal program which will read in a sequence of positive integers, and will print out each value read in followed by the octal representation of its value, using a new line for each pair of equivalent values.

5.7.3

Using the definitions:

(i) f is a factor of n if $(n \bmod f = 0)$ and $(1 < f < n)$.
(ii) A prime number is a number having no factors.

Write a simple Pascal program to output the first 50 primes.

5.7.4

Construct a trace table for program 5.7.2 using the data values:

    0,   127,   43.

5.7.5

Construct a trace table for program 5.7.3, up until the output of the first five primes.

5.7.6

Write a Pascal program to read in a sequence of real numbers and calculate their sum, mean, and mean of the sum of their squares.

5.7.7

Write a Pascal program to find how many terms of the series $1 + 1/2 + 1/3 + \ldots + 1/n$ are required for the sum to exceed five.

5.7.8

Write a loop to evaluate:

$b[1]$ and $b[2]$ and $\ldots$ and $b[10]$

where b is an array of boolean values.

5.7.9

Write a loop to evaluate

$c[1]$ or $c[2]$ or $\ldots$ or $c[20]$

where c is an array of boolean values.

CHAPTER 6

Waving the rules

'Syntactically, though, it must be clear one cannot change the subject
halfway through, not alter tenses to appease the ear.'

W. H. Auden

6.1 INTRODUCTION

In Chapters 3, 4 and 5, we have introduced the most elementary features of
Pascal. We made do, quite intentionally, with as few features as were consistent
with an introduction to very simple programs. In the course of describing these
features of the language, we were concerned partly with the meaning of each
feature – what it is for, when to use it, its effect; we also described the rules
governing what must be written in Pascal in order to use each feature.

These rules are concerned with the systematic arrangement of the symbols
in the language – the order which must be followed for the valid construction
of declarations and instructions, and the way in which declarations and instructions must be arranged in a valid Pascal program. These rules constitute the
syntax of the language. Thus syntax is not *directly* concerned with the meaning
of language. An example given by Noam Chomsky which illustrates the difference
between syntax and meaning is the English sentence:

'Colourless, green ideas sleep furiously.'

This sentence is syntactically correct, even though it does not have a sensible
meaning. Describing syntax rules in English is verbose and imprecise. It is much
easier to describe them by using notations which have been invented specially
for the purpose. Using such notations, a concise presentation of the rules can be
made, thus providing a short and definitive reference which can be used to
check the validity of any piece of program which is in doubt. Such reference is
especially useful when trying to remedy syntax errors detected in a program by
the Pascal compiler, since the information it gives is usually limited to marking
the point in the program at which it *detected* the error, and an error message
of only a few words. Such a message is normally couched in terms whose special
meaning is defined by the syntax rules. Without some familiarity with these
rules, it is difficult to make sense of the message.

There are two formal methods now in common use for clearly expressing
the syntax rules of programming languages. One method uses a slightly extended
form of the notation first popularised by J. M. Backus and Peter Naur when

they used it to define the syntax of the programming language Algol, in 1958. Since then, this notation has been called Backus Naur Form, shortened to BNF. The other formal method for expressing syntax rules uses diagrams rather like flow charts, and these are called *syntax diagrams*. Both BNF and syntax diagrams are used to define the syntax of Pascal in the 'User Manual and Report' written by Kathleen Jensen and Niklaus Wirth. Professor Wirth was the designer of the Pascal language, and the diagrams have been popularised by his use of them. They have come to be known as *Wirth Syntax Diagrams*.

6.2 BACKUS NAUR FORM

We start with an example of the rules defining a valid identifier. These were given in Section 1.8 in English. In BNF the first rule is expressed as follows:

<IDENTIFIER> ::= <LETTER> { <LETTER OR DIGIT> }

The BNF symbol '::=' means 'may consist of', or more shortly, 'is'.

The enclosing pointed brackets '<' and '>' are used in Pascal to mean 'less than', and are not used as brackets at all. In BNF their meaning is quite different. They are used as brackets to indicate that they enclose not symbols which occur literally in Pascal, but the *name* of some language element which occurs in Pascal. This distinction between a language element and the name of such an element is vital. The difference is emphasised by using capital letters for names, and small italic letters for symbols when possible. Of course, some symbols, such as digits or operator symbols, do not contain letters. The overriding distinction is the use of pointed brackets.

The curly brackets '{' and '}' in BNF mean that whatever is enclosed by them may be either omitted altogether, or may occur any number of times, once or more, repeatedly.

To complete the rules for identifiers we need the following two BNF rules:

<LETTER OR DIGIT> ::= <LETTER> | <DIGIT>
 <LETTER>   ::= A|B|C|D|E|F|G|H|I|J|K|L|M|N|O|P
                          |Q|R|S|T|U|V|W|X|Y|Z
                          |a|b|c|d|e|f|g|h|i|j|k|l|m|n|o|p
                          |q|r|s|t|u|v|w|x|y|z
 <DIGIT>   ::= 0|1|2|3|4|5|6|7|8|9

The vertical bar '|' in BNF means 'or'; it simply indicates a choice between alternatives. Note that the choices occurring on the right-hand side of the last two rules are not enclosed in pointed brackets. They are *actual symbols* used in Pascal. The square brackets '[' and ']' indicate a single, optional occurrence of whatever is enclosed by them.

As a second example here are the syntax rules for repetitive statements (that is, loops) in Pascal:

```
<REPETITIVE STATEMENT> ::= <WHILE STATEMENT>
                            | <REPEAT STATEMENT>
                            | <FOR STATEMENT>
<WHILE STATEMENT>   ::= while <EXPRESSION> do <STATEMENT>
<REPEAT STATEMENT> ::= repeat <STATEMENT { ; <STATEMENT>}
                         until <EXPRESSION>
<FOR STATEMENT>     ::= for <CONTROL VARIABLE> := <FOR LIST>
                         do <STATEMENT>
<FOR LIST>          ::=  <INITIAL VALUE> to <FINAL VALUE>
                         | <INITIAL VALUE> downto <FINAL VALUE>
<CONTROL VARIABLE> ::= <IDENTIFIER>
<INITIAL VALUE>     ::= <EXPRESSION>
<FINAL VALUE>       ::= <EXPRESSION>
```

As already pointed out, the use of BNF is not restricted to defining the syntax of Pascal. It may be used to define any formal language. As a third example of its use, we define a very limited formal language which is actually a subset of English. It might conceivably be included in guide books for overseas visitors or tourists in England. The language is called 'Railway-Carriage English', and the syntax rules define it as follows:

```
<CONVERSATION> ::=  { <ASSERTION>[<RESPONSE>]}
<ASSERTION>     ::=  <ADJECTIVE> <NOUN>
<ADJECTIVE>     ::=  lovely | fine |
                     dreadful | dreary | changeable
<NOUN>          ::=  weather
<RESPONSE>      ::=  do you think so? | oh yes |
                     could be worse | marvellous |
                     for the time of year | mmmm
```

6.3 WIRTH SYNTAX DIAGRAMS

A syntax diagram may be thought of as a flow chart representation of a program to recognise a particular language form. The following examples each give a syntax diagram and its BNF equivalent.

Identifier

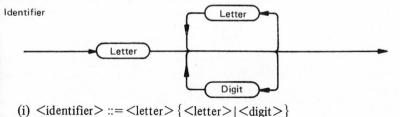

(i) <identifier> ::= <letter> { <letter> | <digit>}

Case Statement

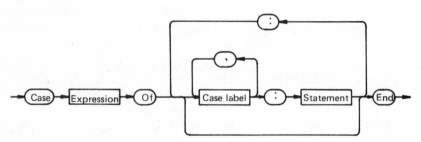

(ii) <case statement> ::= **case** <expression> **of**
                              <case list element> { ; <case list element> } **end**
       <case list element> ::= <case label list> : <statement> | <empty>
       <case label list>   ::= <case label> { , <case label> }

If Statement

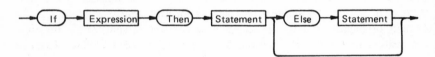

(iii) <if statement> ::= **if** <expression> **then** <statement>
                         | **if** <expression> **then** <statement> **else** <statement>

The use of two different shapes of boxes in the syntax diagrams is important. The rectangular box corresponds to the use of the enclosing brackets
< and > in BNF. A rectangular box encloses the *name* of a Pascal language
element, whereas a round box encloses symbols which actually occur in Pascal,
not their names.

Set

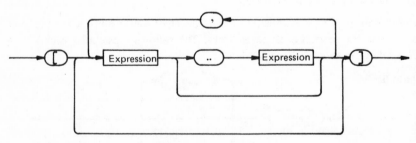

(iv) <set>   ::= [<element list>]
       <element list> ::= <element> { , <element> } | <empty>
       <element>   ::= <expression> | <expression> .. <expression>

6.4 PEDIGREES

t is useful to be able to check whether a piece of program is syntactically correct, and this can be done in an informal way by looking at the appropriate syntax diagram. However, this informal method is liable to error. Sometimes, even when we know something is wrong, because we have received a rude message from the compiler, it is difficult to spot the exact error, unless we use a formal routine checking method.

It is a straightforward matter to show that a piece of program is syntactically well bred by producing its pedigree. Like the pedigree of a well-bred dog or cat, his takes the form of a family tree as shown in Fig. 6.1.

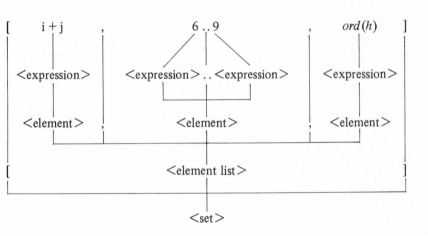

Fig. 6.1 – This pedigree shows that $[i + j, 6..9, ord(h)]$ is a well bred example of $<set>$.

6.5 NEW STYLE BNF

There have been so many different extensions of the original BNF, that a working group of the British Standards Institute has recently proposed that a standard should be defined and adopted. To this end, they have already published a paper, 'The need for a standard' (BSI Committee DPS/13, Working Group on Syntactic Languages). Their paper contains a proposal for a new standard which seems to be an important step forward toward that goal. The notation they propose has greater clarity and flexibility than that used in the Pascal Report, and it has therefore been adopted for use in this book.

The main ideas are similar. The square bracket and curly bracket symbols, and the vertical bar have the same meaning as they have in earlier versions of BNF; but the double colon followed by an equals sign is replaced simply by the equals sign, with the same meaning.

The greatest change is the abolition of angle brackets '<' and '>' to enclose names of symbols (or classes of symbols). These names now stand by themselves, without being enclosed by any kind of brackets. Any name containing more than one word has its word components hyphenated together. But symbols which actually occur in the language whose syntax is being defined must now be enclosed in quotes, for example, rewriting example (iii) of Section 6.3 gives:

if-statement = 'if' expression 'then' statement
                    | 'if' expression 'then' statement
                    'else' statement;

Each syntax rule is terminated by a semicolon.

The main advantages of the new notation are:

(i) A symbol which is used both in the syntax rules and in the language being defined is now easily distinguished in its two different roles, by the use of quotation marks. Thus, square brackets without quotes denote optional occurrence of what they enclose, whereas square brackets within quotes are literals.

(ii) The use of quotation marks instead of angle brackets is far more natural and therefore easier to understand.

The complete syntax of Pascal is given in Appendix B, both in new-style BNF, and in the form of syntax diagrams.

6.6 PROBLEMS

6.6.1

Draw the syntax diagrams for 'Railway-Carriage English'.

6.6.2

Construct the pedigrees of:

(i) **repeat** $k := k + 1$ **while** $k < 100$;
(ii) **repeat** $k := k + 1$ **until** $k > 100$;
(iii) **if** $x > y$ **then do** $y := x$;

6.6.3

Construct an example of a valid <conversation> in 'Railway-Carriage English'.

CHAPTER 7

Data types and data structure

> 'The time has come,' the Walrus said,
> 'To talk of many things:
> Of shoes — and ships — and sealing wax —
> Of cabbages — and kings —'
>
> Lewis Carroll

7.1 DO YOU KNOW WHAT YOU CAN DO WITH YOUR DATA?

The *type* of a variable denotes the domain of values associated with it (see Section 1.3). Another aspect of type may be seen by considering the particular set of operations one may carry out upon values of a particular type. If r and s are of type *integer*, then an expression such as r or s is meaningless. Similarly p/q is meaningless for *boolean* p, q; and x div y is meaningless for *real* x, y.

Even operations we are accustomed to think of as identical for two different types, such as multiplication for reals and integers, are actually different operations. Integer multiplication gives an exact result, but real multiplication gives an approximate result. (The approximate nature of all operations with reals was discussed in Section 2.3.3–2.3.5.). For example, the approximate nature of *real* values makes the '=' relation an extremely uncertain one whose result is largely a matter of chance. The following program is merely one of many which can be constructed to illustrate the point being made. The results shown here were obtained when the program ran on a CDC 6600 machine, and they are, of course, entirely machine-dependent.

```
program realarith(output);
var a, b, x, y : real;
    k : integer;
begin {illustration 1}
    a := 1;
    b := 3;
    for k := 1 to 4 do
        begin
            a := a + 2;
            b := b + 2;
            x := a/b;
            x := 1/x;
            y := b/a;
            if x = y
```

```
        then writeln(' equal values equal')
        else  writeln(' dif between equal values =', x − y)
    end;
writeln;
{illustration 2}
x := 1/3;
y := 1/3;
    for k := 2 to 5 do
        begin
        x := x*y;
        a := exp(k*ln(y));
            if x = a
            then writeln(' equal values equal')
            else  writeln(' dif between equal values =', x − a)
        end
end.
```

Output:

dif between equal values = 7.1054273576010E−015
equal values equal
equal values equal
equal values equal
equal values equal
equal values equal
dif between equal values = 5.5511151231258E−017
dif between equal values = 2.7755575615629E−017

The purpose of showing the foregoing program and its output is to drive home two points, one of them particular, and the other general.

(i) Never rely on the result of an equality test between reals. Your purpose may be served instead by using a test to see if their *relative* difference is very small, for example:

$$abs((x − y)/(x + y)) < epsilon$$

(ii) Every operator is defined uniquely for one and only one *type* of value. This is true even though we sometimes use the same representation for two different operators, for example '*' for multiplication both on reals and on integers.

7.2 SIMPLE TYPES WITH ABSOLUTELY PRECISE VALUES

In Pascal, *integer* is not the only type with operations which yield *absolutely precise* results. Variables of type *boolean* have the same property. A third type having the property of absolute precision is the type *char*.

The values of *type* char are a set of characters. This set always includes the complete alphabetically ordered set of capital Latin letters A...Z, the complete numerically ordered set of decimal digits 0...9, and the blank character. It usually contains other characters, such as:

$$+ - * / ( ) = , . ;$$

and often contains others, such as:

$$[\,] <> \leqslant \geqslant \, ' \{ \}$$

but there is no standard set, and no standard number of characters in the set. This is dependent upon the hardware (computing equipment) at particular computer centres, as does the particular ordering of any such set. However, each set is always finite, and has a defined ordering.

The ordering of the character set determines the results yielded by a standard function called *chr*, whose operand must always be a value of type *integer*. The function *chr* is a data-transfer function which maps from integers to characters. If k is a non-negative integer then $chr(k)$ yields a result of type *char*. This result is the character whose ordering correponds to the integer value k. For values of k which are too high, or negative, no result exists for $chr(k)$.

Another transfer function, *ord*, operates on a precise-value of type either *char* or *boolean*, and yields an *integer* result, for example:

$$ord(false) = 0$$
$$ord(true) = 1$$

With *char* type operands, the result is machine-dependent, but, for example, on a CDC 6600 computer:

$$ord('4') = 31$$
$$ord('Z') = 26$$
$$ord('+') = 37$$

Two more standard functions, the predecessor and sucessor functions, *pred* and *succ*, are defined for all precise-value types. Each function yields a result which is determined by the ordering of values within each type. If k is a variable of precise-value type, then

(i) $pred(k)$ is defined provided $ord(k) > 0$.
(ii) $ord(pred(k)) = ord(k) - 1$.
(iii) $ord(succ(k)) = ord(k) + 1$.
(iv) $pred(succ(k)) = succ(pred(k)) = k$.
(v) $succ(k)$ is defined provided $ord(k) < maxint$.

The relational operators such as $>$, $<$, $=$ may be applied to values within any precise-value type, using the ordering of values within that type. For example, the *boolean* values *true* and *false* are ordered so that *true* $>$ *false*. Characters are alphabetically ordered, and therefore

$$'A' < 'B' < 'C' < \ldots < 'Z'.$$

7.3 STANDARD AND NON-STANDARD SIMPLE TYPES

7.3.1 Standard types

We have now discussed all the simple standard types and may classify them as follows:

precise-value type: *integer*
                             char
                             boolean
approximate-value type: *real*

In addition to the standard types, other, new types may be defined by the programmer and declared in a Pascal program. Such declarations define the ordering of the sets of values which constitute the new types.

7.3.2 Scalar types

The syntactic form of declaration of a scalar type is as follows:

'**type**' type-identifier '=' '(' identifier { ',' identifer } ')' ';';

EXAMPLE:

type *sex* = (*female, male*);
        day = (*mon, tue, wed, thu, fri, sat, sun*);

The type *boolean*, which is in fact a standard type, has a definition which, in this form, is as follows:

type *boolean* = (*false, true*);

All standard operators and functions which can be applied to simple precise-value standard types can be applied equally well to non-standard types of this kind, for example:

ord(*female*) = 0
ord(*thur*) = 3
(*thur* $>$ *fri*) = *false*
pred(*wed*) = *tue*
succ(*female*) = *male*
(*male* = *female*) = *false*
ord(*male* = *female*) = 0

7.3.3 Subrange types

The programmer may also define a new type whose domain of values is a sub-range of the domain of any other precise-value simple type. The definition of a subrange indicates the least and largest constant value in the subrange. The declaration for a subrange type has the form:

   type type-identifier '=' constant '. .' constant ';';

EXAMPLES:

   type *workday* = *mon . . fri* {subrange of day};
        index = 1 . . 100 {subrange of integer};
        letter = $'a' . . 'z'$ {subrange of character};
        digit = $'0' . . '9'$ {subrange of character};

The use of scalar and subrange types helps the writing of programs which are easy to read, and whose meaning is clear and self-explanatary.

7.4 DATA WITH STRUCTURE – ARRAYS

7.4.1 Introducing arrays

All the data types we have met so far are *simple* types, and a classified summary of them is:

simple types:	standard types:	approximate-value	*real*
		precise value	*integer*
			char
			boolean
	non-standard types:	user-defined scalar types	
		subrange types	

Any value of a simple type is called simple because it is a single quantity. Very often, the data we wish to process cannot properly be regarded as a mere collection of single quantities. It is characterised by the presence of interelations of a fundamental nature between different quantities. Some of these interelations are relatively simple: others are more complex. All levels of interelations are characterised when we say that the data is structured. In order that our programs may more directly reflect the operations we wish to carry out, we need the facility of defining data types which themselves are structured. In Pascal, we can define structures which model the interelations of our data by making declarations which build structured types from the components provided by the simple types we have already discussed.

   An **array** type is a structure consisting of a fixed number of *components*, each component being of the same type. Each element (component) of an array is designated by an *index*, and can be denoted and directly accessed by the array identifier followed by a value of *index* type enclosed within square brackets. The declaration for an array type has the form:

> **type** <type identifier> = **array** [<index type>{, <index type>}]
>   **of** <component type>';';

EXAMPLES:

> **type** *onedeearray*1   = **array** [1 .. 10] **of** *char*;
> **type** *onedeearray*2   = **array** ['a' .. 'z'] **of** *boolean*;
> **type** *twodeearray*1   = **array** [1..3,1...3] **of** *real*;
> **type** *threedeearray*1 = **array** [1..2,1..4,1..3] **of** *integer*;
> **type** *array*3   = **array** [*char*] **of** *char*;

The choice of index type is restricted. It must be of type *char*, *boolean*, a user-defined scalar type, or a subrange type. It cannot be of type *real*; nor can it be of (unbounded range) type *integer*.

7.4.2 Simple programs using arrays

{program *coder*1 is a program which reads 10 characters from the input file and outputs them in a coded form. The code is stored in an array which is used as a look-up table. The code used is a simple-minded one which maps 'a' to 'z', etc.}

```
program coder1 (input, output);
type table = array [char] of char;
var code : table;
    k : integer;
    s, ch : char;
begin
  {set up look-up table of codes}
    for s := 'a' to 'z' do
      code [s] := char(ord('a') + ord('z') − ord(s));
  {do encoding, using look-up table}
    for k := 1 to 10 do
      begin
        read(ch);
        writeln(' ',ch,'    ',code[ch])
      end;
  writeln
end.
```

Note that type declarations must always come before variable declarations in any program containing both kinds of declaration.

Note also that, for reasons given in Section 11.8.1, any line of output which starts with a string or with a variable of type *char* must include an initial blank, otherwise the first character output on that line will be lost.

The next program, *maxandpos*, finds the maximum value in an array and its position in the array

```
program maxandpos(input, output);
var max, pos, k : integer;
    a : array [1..20] of integer;
begin
  {first, read in 20 data values to the array}
    for k := 1 to 20 do
      begin
        read(a[k]);
        writeln(a[k])
      end;
    max := a[1];
    pos := 1;
    for k : 2 to 20 do
      begin
        if a[k] > max
        then
            begin
              pos := k;
              max := a[pos]
            end
      end;
      writeln(' max value =', max,', position =', pos)
end.
```

if the data input to this program is

37	−153	1	0	45
1072	3	5	11	−1
22	47	8	11	19
17	18	−4	2	5

then the output is max value = 1072, position = 6}

{The next program, *simplesort*, reads in an array of integer values and sorts it into ascending order. The method of sorting used is just about the most simple to program, but is very inefficient; hence is should be used only for sorting very small arrays}

```
program simplesort(input, output);
var k, last, max, pos, temp : integer;
    a : array [1..10] of integer;
begin
    {Method is to find the max and swap it with the last element, and keep
    repeating this for the remaining array not including the last element}
fork := 1 to 10 do
    begin
        read(a[k]);
        writeln(k, a[k])
    end;
{Now sort the data}
for last := 10 downto 2 do
    begin
        pos  := 1;
        max := a[pos];
            for k := 2 to last do
                begin {find max element}
                    if a[k] > max
                    then
                        begin
                            pos  := k;
                            max := a[pos]
                        end;
                    {now swap}
                    a[pos] := a[last];
                    a[last] := max
                end
    end;
            {Now print out sorted array}
            for k := 1 to 10 do
            writeln(k, a[k])
end.
```

The study of sorting methods is well-developed, but is better dealt with in more advanced texts. For searching a list of items which has already been sorted, there is an efficient method called binary search. This method is commonly used in finding an entry in a dictionary. It consists of opening the dictionary (about halfway through). If the word required lies in the right-hand half of the dictionary then regard the dictionary as reduced in size to the right-hand half and start again; if in the left-hand half, then similarly, the process being repeated until the word is found.

The following program, *binsearch*, stores 100 items of data, already sorted,
an array R. It then reads in individual items, and reports whether each is
ᴜded in the array, and if so, gives its position. The program terminates when
gative item is read in.

```
program binsearch(input, output);
var a : array [1..100] of integer;
    middle, lower, upper, wanted, k : integer;
    found : boolean;
begin
  for k := 1 to 100 do a [k] := 3*k;
    lower := 1;
    upper := 100;
    {sorted data has now been stored. Now read in wanted values, and
    search, until a negative value is read in}
    read(wanted) :
      while wanted >= 0 do
        begin
          lower  := 1;
          upper  := 100;
          found := false;
          repeat
                middle := (upper + lower)div 2;
                  if a [middle] = wanted
                  then found := true
                  else if a [middle] > wanted
                       then upper := middle−1
                       else lower := middle+1
          until found or (lower > upper);
          if found
          then writeln(' found', wanted, 'at position', middle)
          else writeln(wanted, 'not found');
          read(wanted)
        end
end.
```

3 When and how to use arrays

have seen several examples of the use of an array in a program, and can now
ꜱe to consider its general characteristics as a data structure.

(i) Every component of an array is the same type.
(ii) Every component of an array is equally accessible by means of its
   index. An *index* may be computed. By means of an index we can make

random access to the data in an array. We are not obliged to read sequentially through it to find a required component of data.

(iii) If we do not require random access to our data, but can process it sequentially, then we do not need to store it in an array, but can process it, one component at a time, reading it from a sequential file.

(iv) The definition of an array specifies both the component type and the index type.

7.4.4 Declaring arrays

Note that there are two ways of going about the declaration of arrays. We have already seen examples of both methods. The first method declares a new, user defined type, giving this type a name, (see examples in Section 7.4.1). Such type definitions can be followed by variable declarations which use the name of the new type to specify the type of the variable(s), (see program *coder*1, Section 7.4.2). The second method does not declare a new type by name, but specifies the type of the structured variable in full detail, as in the programs *maxandpos, simplesort*, and *binsearch* (Section 7.4.2).

The advantage of the first method is that it is more compact if several variables of the same new type are to be declared. If only one is to be declared, then the second method is more compact.

Note that all **type** declarations must come before any **var** declarations in a program.

7.5 REPRESENTATION OF DATA

7.5.1 Constants

We defined constants in Chapter 1, and examples of them occurred in Sections 1.4 and 4.1, so that we have met constants of type, *real, integer, boolean,* and 'character-string'. All the constants we have seen until now in programs have had values which are plainly evident, for example:

true, false, 3.14159265, 7,
'*abcdef*', '*small is beautiful*'

Sometimes it is more convenient to use a symbolic name (that is, an identifier) for a constant, just as is done for a variable. The value denoted by a constant identifier is of course not plainly evident, and must therefore be made evident in programs by means of a *constant definition*. Examples of such definitions are:

(i) **const** *pi* = 3.1415926536;
(ii) **const** *farenheitzero* = 32;
(iii) **const** *line*1 = 'This is the house that Jack built';
(iv) **const** *a* = 2; *b* = 2.777; *c* = 'hello';
   separator = '******************';

There are advantages in using a symbolic name to denote a constant value:

(i) Even though the value is not evident, a meaningful name may be chosen which has more obvious significance than the value itself.

(ii) However many times the identifier is used in a program, its value is defined once and for all in the constant definition. This minimises the possibility of error. It also facilitates the global change of such a value at a single stroke.

(iii) In some cases the identifer may be shorter than the value it denotes. This is often the case when string constants are concerned.

Examples of constant definitions have already been given. The syntax rule for a constant definition requires that it always take the form:

'**const**' identifier '=' constant';' {identifier '=' constant ';'};

Syntax rules require also that where a program block contains any or all of:

constant definitions
type definitions
variable definitions

they shall occur in that order.

7.5.2 Character-strings and packed arrays

In Section 7.4.2, in program *coder*1, we saw an example of an array of *char*. In this example, each element of the array was a variable of type *char*, that is, a variable whose value was a single character. If we are processing large numbers of characters, it saves storage space to *pack* characters together more densely, so that a single variable holds a string instead of a single character. If we are concerned with processing strings rather than single characters it may even be more convenient to use such packed arrays of characters. A *string* is in fact nothing more than a packed array of *char*. However, *string* is not a predeclared standard type as are *real, integer, boolean,* and *char*. This is because such a predefinition would have to fix the length, that is, the number of characters, in a string. Such choice would be arbitrary, and is therefore left to the programmer, who is free to declare strings of various lengths, for example:

```
type
    string10 = packed array [1..10] of char;
    string20 = packed array [1..20] of char;
    string30 = packed array [1..30] of char;
var
    name1, name2, name3 : string10;
    doublename1, doublename2 : string20;
    triplename1 : string30;
```

It is vital to note that strings of different length are of different type. A string of length say 8 chars cannot be assigned therefore to a variable whose type is *string*10. This difficulty can be overcome by 'padding out' the 8 chars by the addition of two blank chars at the end, thereby increasing the length.

7.6 PROBLEMS

7.6.1

Write a program to read in pairs of positive (non-zero) integers, and to calculate the greatest common divisor for each pair, printing out all three values with appropriate captions. The program should stop if it reads in a data value which is zero or negative.

Use the following method: Divide the larger integer by the smaller. If there is no remainder then the divisor is the answer; otherwise substitute the remainder for the larger integer and start again. (This method is known as Euclid's algorithm.)

7.6.2

Write a program which reads in integers in the range 0 to 15, and prints out the value of each integer followed by its hexadecimal representation. The program stops when it reads in a data value which is out of range.

7.6.3

Write a program which does the same as that in Section 7.6.2, but which deals with integers in the range 0 to 256.

7.6.4

Write a pair of programs which code and decode English text, using the following coding techniques (which upset frequency expectations):

   (i) Every occurrence of the word 'the' is coded into a single character.
   (ii) A set of five characters is reserved into any one of which the letter 'e' is coded. (The five may be taken one at a time in turn.)
   (iii) Each other letter and punctuation mark is coded into a character belonging to the set of letters, digits and other graphic symbols available
   (iv) Each occurrence of one or more spaces is coded into a single character and the character used for this is drawn from any one of the remaining unused characters, taken in turn, as for the letter 'e'.

The programs should be tested by presenting suitable data to the coder presenting it's output to the decoder, and comparing with the original input How should they be expected to differ if at all?

5

e a program which reads in a set of nine integers and stores them in some
which conveniently represents the first three as the first row, the second
e as the second row and the third three as the third row of a 3 × 3 square
. The program should test to see whether the integer sum of all three rows,
ree columns and the two diagonals are equal. The integers should be printed
in suitable layout, and if the sums are equal, the words 'magic square' should
rinted, followed by the value of a row sum, otherwise the words 'dull
re'.

6

e a program which reads nine integers into a 3 × 3 array, prints the array in
ble layout, then interchanges each row with corresponding column, and
ts out the resulting (transposed) array. If the transposed array is identical
the original array the program should print the word 'symmetric', otherwise
ymmetric'.

7

e a program which reads in two 3 × 3 matrices, prints them out, and prints
their product (that is, each element of the product matrix is the inner
uct of the corresponding row and column of the first and second matrices
ectively).
Test your program on the following data. In each case use for the first
ix the values:

1 2 3
4 5 6
7 8 9

the second matrix use:

(i)	1 0 0	(ii)	0 0 1	(iii)	0 1 0	(iv)	1 0 0
	0 1 0		0 1 0		1 0 0		0 0 1
	0 0 1		1 0 0		0 0 1		0 1 0

product should be unchanged by (i), but (ii) should interchange columns
d 3, (iii) should interchange columns 1 and 2, while (iv) should interchange
mns 2 and 3.

CHAPTER 8

Exploiting the power of the array

φαλανξ (phalanx) — The Macedonian battle order used with such success by
Alexander the Great: a body of heavy-armed infantry drawn up in close array
to form a square, with spears overlapping and shields joined to form a roof
and walls.

.1 INTRODUCTION

The array is a powerful piece of organisation, and not only for data. It should
be noted that 'array' is the opposite of 'disarray'. In this sense, 'array' and
'order' are synonymous, and if we think of a one-dimensional array, its main
feature is that its components are ordered, with the result that we can utilise
this order as an index which gives immediate access at random to any component
of the array. If this property — order, appears as an obvious and simple property
of a one-dimensional array, a multi-dimensional array fairly bristles with it.

For example, a two-dimensional array presents two different equally
obvious orderings — we may take the components one by one, row by row, or
column by column; and there are other less obvious implicit orderings such as
those along the diagonals. We can always easily map the components of any
array onto a simple linear structure, that is, one-dimensional array; and there
is usually a relatively wide choice of such mappings.

Intelligent use of the array enables us to structure our data in such a way as
to construct a computer model of the information we wish to process. Careful
design of a model requires extraction of the essential features and relationships
which may be partly obscured by other less relevant information. By constructing a simplified model we emphasise the relations which are relevant to
the processing we wish to carry out. This greatly eases the task of applying an
algorithm to the problem we have to solve, and the net result is the program we
require. To quote Niklaus Wirth:

'Algorithms + Data Structures = Programs'.

However, for the moment, we wish to concentrate upon the data structures
rather than upon the algorithms. Each component of an array has an index and
a value. It is helpful to visualise it as a box containing a value, with an index
number outside the box (rather like the number on a front door). Because the
index is itself a value, this can be stored in another box, and we can exploit this
idea as follows. Suppose we have an array whose values we want to be able to
process in ascending order of magnitude. One thing we could do would be to

sort the array by interchanging the values in the boxes until they were stored in the order required. The box with index 1 would then hold the smallest value, the next smallest would be in 2, and so on. An alternative to actually moving the values about to obtain this order is to leave them in their original positions and to use a second array whose values will be used as links pointing to the index numbers of the first array. To do this, we also need a simple variable which we can call *first*, which holds the value of the index of the smallest component value in the original array. Suppose that index is 15, then in box 15 of our second, *link* array, we should store the index number of the next smallest number, say 27 (see Fig. 8.1). Proceeding in this way, we can set up a chain of links threading a whole array in the order required (Fig. 8.2).

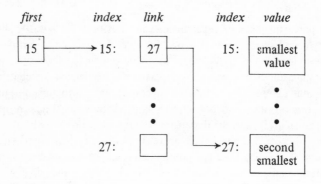

Fig. 8.1.

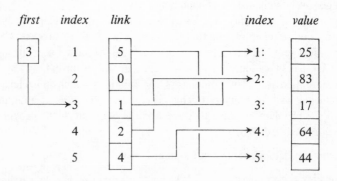

Fig. 8.2 – Picture of an array threaded by a chain of links held in a second array.

This technique can be extended. We might have an array of values which we want to split into two classes which we process in different ways. For example, the values might be amounts owed by customers, and we might want to link into chain all those who are dealt with by salesman A, and into a separate chain, all those dealt with by salesman B. (In this case we may not be concerned with the order within each chain.) As we have two chains, we need a variable for each of the two to hold the index number of the first link in the chain, and we can call these *firstA* and *firstB*. The last link in the chain, having no index to point to, is given the value zero.

In the picture of an array with two chains (Fig. 8.3), salesman A has customers with index numbers 1, 2, 5 and 8, while salesman B has those with index numbers 3, 4, 6 and 7. We see that *firstA* holds the value 1, which is the index of the first customer belonging to A, and *firstB* holds the value 3, the index of the first customer belonging to B. The last link in each chain is again given the value zero. This is an abritrary but convenient convention denoting there are no further links in the chain.

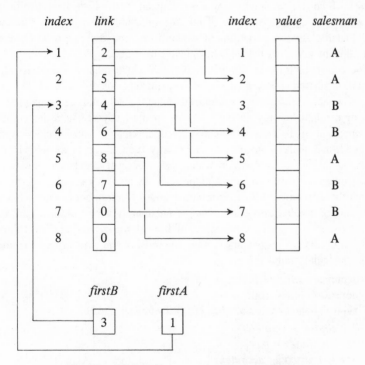

Fig. 8.3 – Picture of an array threaded by two chains,
one starting in *firstA* and the other starting in *firstB*.

The reader should work through the chain of links in the diagrams, in which the arrows indicate the index pointed at by each link value, before proceeding to the next section. In the case study which follows, the technique just described is fully exploited. Our attention is to be directed here less to some particular problem than to a picture or model which represents a system of entities and relationships which gives rise to a whole number of possible problems. We shall see how we can use the idea of data types together with the types we have already introduced, in particular the array, to describe such a model in terms of Pascal declarations.

8.2 CASE STUDY 1 – ANALYSIS OF EXPENDITURE

A model is required within which we can easily and methodically organise data which represents information relating to expenditure. The information arises as individual transactions. Each transaction has some textual information, for example name of supplier, which we assume is adequately allowed for by a character string of length not greater than 32 characters. In addition there is a date of transaction, amount, and an account code. The account code is a member of a set of codes, each denoting a subdivision into which all expenditure is analysed according to the nature of its purpose. We assume there are not more than 10 such classes or partitions of expenditure, and that the total number of transactions in any given period is not greater than 100.

The problems foreseen are all of the kind which requires some retrieval of information, based upon analysis of expenditure according to the account codes. The actual information required might be of totals and analysed sub-totals, or it might be only partially related to the analysis. The order in time of the occurrence of the transactions may be of interest – seasonal characteristics of expenditure analysis might be sought. Any such enquiries we wish to make must be facilitated by the way in which the storage of data has been organised. This organisation should reflect and preserve as many as possible of the ways in which the different kinds of information about the transactions are related.

In this particular case study, we present merely a possible solution, ready made, without any prior examination of how it was arrived at. The following skeleton program is a framework embodying most of the data structures required for this particular model.

```
program expenditure (input, output);
    constant limit = 100;
    type charfield = packed array [1..32] of char;
         index = 1..limit;
         accindex = 0..9;
    var accountcode : accindex;
        supplier : array [index] of charfield;
        accountname : array [accindex] of charfield;
        total : array [accindex] of integer;
        first, last : array [accindex] of index;
        link : array [index] of index;
        amount, grandtotal : real;
        date, amount : array [index] of integer;
```

{More variable declarations are probably required by the algorithms
which read in the data and perform the analysis processes.}
begin
{Program fragments implementing the processing algorithms required.}
end.

.2.1 Pictorial representation of the arrays in program *expenditure*

The transactions which have been actually entered in the pictorial represen-
ation of the data arrays (Figs. 8.4 and 8.5) are as given in the following trans-
ction records:

index	amount	supplier	accountcode	date
1	£450.50	National Insurers	3	1/6/78
3	£109.56	Brownstone	0	15/6/78
6	£52.00	Perfecta	5	19/6/78
10	£26.00	Perfecta	5	1/7/78
14	£216.32	Curruthers	0	22/8/78
15	£52.32	Borwnstone	0	23/8/78
16	£78.00	Perfecta	5	23/8/78
22	£823.24	Smith	0	20/1/79

Each transaction is identified by a unique key we have called *index*, which is
ndeed used to index each of the arrays *date*, *amount*, *link*, and *supplier* in which
we store the information from the transaction record. This index number is
merely a sequence number given to each transaction in order as it is recorded.

The method shown here of recording the date as a single integer is an
example of data packing. The integer is built up by using the first two (most
significant) digits for the year, the next two for the month, and the last two for
the day of the month. The advantage of packing is to save storage space. The
advantage of packing the data in this order, is that direct comparisons of dates
may be made by one simple arithmetic comparison — a later date is always
represented by a greater integer than an earlier date.

The amount is represented as an integer (in pence). This too may be thought
of as a form of packing.

The account codes are the index values of the account names (see Fig. 8.5).
As there are ten account codes (values 0 to 9), it is more convenient to use an
array called *first* with ten components, one for each account code, than to use
ten separately named variables. In the example in Section 8.1, when there were
only two chains, we used separately named variables *firstA* and *firstB*. The
array *first* is used to record the first transaction under each account code. Before
and until such a transaction occurs, the value of the relevant element of *first* is
initialised to zero. The array *link* is used to construct ten separate chains, linking
all the transactions which belong to the same account code. A separate chain is

Index	Date	Amount	Link	Supplier
1	780601	45050	0	National Insurers
2				
3	780615	10956	14	Brownstone
4				
5				
6	780619	5200	10	Perfecta
7				
8				
9				
10	780701	2600	16	Perfecta
11				
12				
13				
14	780822	21632	15	Carruthers
15	780823	5232	22	Brownstone
16	780823	7800	0	Perfecta
17				
18				
19				
20				
21				
22	790120	82324	0	Smith
23				
24				
25				
•				
•				
•				
100				

Fig. 8.4.

Index	First	Last	Total	Accountname
0	3	22	120144	punched cards
1	0	0	0	equipment repairs
2	0	0	0	equipment rental
3	1	1	45050	insurances
4	0	0	0	software charges
5	6	16	15600	magnetic tapes
6	0	0	0	lineprinter paper
7	0	0	0	lineprinter ribbons
8	0	0	0	PO communications
9	0	0	0	maintenance

Fig. 8.5.

constructed for each account code, and the array *first* is used to record the index of the first link in each chain. When a new transaction is recorded which is the first for its particular account code, the element of *first* whose index is that account code is assigned the value of the index of the transaction.

At the same time, the corresponding component of *total* is updated, by adding to it the appropriate value of *amount*. Also, the component of the array *last* is assigned the value of the transaction index; this is done so that when the next transaction analysed under the same account code occurs, its index value may be assigned to the *link* component for the last transaction having the same account code. In this way the chain is built, link by link. Each component which is currently the last to be added to the chain carries a link value of zero until a new link is added.

The reader should examine the list of transactions, and, taking them one at a time, work through the entries in all the arrays relating to each particular transaction. For example, let us describe this tracing through process for the first transaction:

index	amount	supplier	accountcode	date
1	£450.50	National Insurers	3	1/6/78

The unique key identifying this transaction is its index value, 1. This tells us that each of the components of information it contains – date, amount and supplier, (but not account code) are stored in the corresponding components, that is, index value 1, of the arrays called *date, amount,* and *supplier.* The date 1/6/78 is stored as the value 780601, a single integer representing the date in year, month, day order. The expenditure recorded is classified under the account name *insurances.* The index number of this account name is seen to be 3, and as this is the first record of expenditure under this account name, its index number, 1, is entered in compartment 3 of the array of pointers called *first.* As, for the moment, it is also the last item in this chain, *last*[3] is given the value 1 as well; and *link*[1], its link to the next item in the chain, is given the value 0, meaning no more links. That completes the entries relating to the first recorded transaction.

8.2.2 An expenditure report

Here is a program fragment which accesses the stored information to produce lists of all transactions, analysed under account codes:

```
for accountcode := 0 to 9 do
   begin
      if total [accountcode] > 0 then
         begin
            writeln (accountname [accountcode]);
            index := first [accountcode];
               repeat
                  writeln (date [index], supplier [index], amount [index]);
                  index := link [index];
               until index = 0;
               writeln(' total expended on ', accountname,' = '
                                       , total [accountcode]);
            writeln
         end;
         grandtotal := grandtotal + total [accountcode]
   end;
   writeln (' grandtotal of expenditure =', grandtotal)
```

8.3 CASE STUDY 2 – SELECTION BY SUCCESSIVE ELIMINATION

This is the basis of a game commonly played by children: they stand in a ring and adopt a count-down procedure, the child counted 'out' leaving the ring. This process continues until only one survivor remains. The problem of determining the survivor is sometimes known as the Josephus problem. Josephus was a curious mixture of philosopher, renegade and patriot of ancient Judea at the time of the fall of Jerusalem and the destruction of the Temple by the Romans. According to the story, Josephus and his companions were trapped in a cave by the Romans, and were being starved out. The children's game was played with gruesome reality, the one counted out being expelled from the cave to be cut to pieces by the Roman soldiers, and one by one they were, all except the sole survivor Josephus, who evidently knew a thing or two about the game.

In order to construct a model of the surviving ring (of children or men), we need to store, for each individual, two pieces of information – identity of left neighbour and identity of right neighbour. If each member of the ring is identified by an index, then all we need by way of data structures are two arrays of indexes, one called *left* and the other called *right*. Index is here a sub-range of the integers, from 1 to the original number of members of the ring, say n. In this model, the right neighbour is the successor and the left neighbour the predecessor for each member. To complete the ring, the nth member is regarded as the left neighbour (or predecessor) of the first, and therefore also, the 1st member as the right neighbour (or successor) of the nth.

The count-down procedure may be arbitrarily chosen, and, in the illustrative program fragments which follow, we have chosen a count down of three for simplicity.

8.3.1 program heading

```
program Josephus (input, output);
constant n = 20 {say};
type index = 1..n;
var leftneighbour, rightneighbour : array [index] of index;
    start, k, count, hit, survivor : index;
```

8.3.2 initialisation of ring

```
leftneighbour[1] := n;
rightneighbour[n] := 1;
    for k := 1 to n − 1 do
      begin
        leftneighbour[k + 1] := k;
        rightneighbour[k] := k + 1
      end;
    {ring initialised}
```

8.3.3 {countdown process, beginning with the member whose index is the value of *start*}

```
for k := 1 to 3 do
    start := rightneighbour[start];
    hit   := start;
    start := rightneighbour[start];
```

8.3.4 {elimination process, that is, elimination from the ring of the member whose index is *hit*}

> *rightneighbour* [*leftneighbour* [*hit*]] := *rightneighbour* [*hit*];
> *leftneighbour* [*rightneighbour* [*hit*]] := *leftneighbour* [*hit*];

8.3.5 {test to see whether all the eliminations have been completed}

> **if** *leftneighbour* [*start*] = *start*
> **and** *rightneighbour* [*start*] = *start*
> **then**
> > {eliminations are completed and survivor is member whose index is current value of start}
> **else**
> > {continue with the countdown process followed by the elimination process}

8.4 PROBLEMS

8.4.1

A platoon of 60 infantrymen has been drilled to come on parade in a single line and to number off from 1 to 60. At the command 'Rank 6' they form into 6 rows of 10. At the command 'Rank 5', they reform into 5 rows of 12. In each case, on the command 'Refile', they reform into a single line by each row following onto the one in front, and preserving the original numbered order.

Write expressions for *row* and *column* for man number k after each of the commands 'Rank 6' and 'Rank 5'.

8.4.2

Write the program fragment which reads in and stores the data for program *expenditure*. Make and state concisely and clearly in the form of a comment any format requirements to which the data is expected to conform.

8.4.3

Write a program fragment for program *expenditure* which extracts for one account code the four quarterly totals of expenditure covering months 1-3, 4-6, 7-9, and 10-12.

8.4.4

Write a complete program to solve the Josephus problem for an initial ring of 30 members, using a countdown of 3 the first time, but thereafter each countdown is to be set to the value of the index of the member just hit.

CHAPTER 9

Sub-programs

Left sleeve: Follow the instructions for right sleeve, reading *k.* for *p.* and *p.* for *k.*

Vogue knitting book

9.1 INTRODUCTION

In Section 5.5 we discussed how to approach the problem of writing a simple program, simple in the sense that its flow of control is uncomplicated, and in the sense that it is short, say less than twenty lines. In Sections 8.2 and 8.3 we introduced programs of much less simplicity. Not only were they longer, but we saw the beginnings of some complexity of structure, both in the actual algorithms and in the organisation of their data. In order to cope with these complications in Section 8.3 we discussed and examined fragments of programs rather than entire programs.

When planning to write a non-trivial program it is vital at the start not to plunge into the mass of detail involved, but rather to rise above it and take a birds-eye view of the program. This can be achieved by attacking the organisation of the program at the crudest possible level first, and then, step by step, making refinements. The selection of 'program fragments' in Section 8.3 was a selection of main tasks to be accomplished in the program. If such fragments are given names, they may be regarded as sub-programs and, before they are worked out in any detail, the main program may be specified in terms of sub-programs. Such a specification constitutes a first level of refinement of the program into constituent parts, which themselves are partial programs.

To turn a partial program into a sub-program implies giving it a form of some kind which has a certain completeness. The various programming languages provide differing facilities for doing just this, and use various names for the resulting forms:

    subroutine,
    routine,
    function,
    procedure,
    process,
    etc.

We use the term sub-program as a programming language-independent generalisation to encompass all of these.

9.2 FUNCTIONS

A mathematical function may be regarded as a certain kind of sub-program. In Pascal, and in many other programming languages, sub-programs for calculating the values to be returned by some of the more commonly used mathematical functions are provided, ready-made in the form of standard functions. For example the function $sin(x)$ maps the variable x from the domain of *all* reals to a real *codomain* bounded by -1 and $+1$.

Any computable function is determined by a domain, a codomain, and a terminating algorithm which provides a mapping from domain to codomain. In programming terminology, the variable x of a function $f(x)$ is called its argument, or more commonly a parameter of the function. All the standard functions in Pascal are functions of a single variable. They can have only one parameter. However, we frequently meet and wish to use functions which are *not* standard functions. Such functions may have more than one parameter, for example, the diagonal of a rectangular solid whose sides are of length u, v, w may be expressed as the function:

$$diag(u, v, w) = \sqrt{(u^2 + v^2 + w^2)}$$

where u, v, w are integers and non-negative and the value returned by the function *diag* is real and non-negative, that is, the codomain of *diag* is the set of real non-negative numbers. If we wish, we may extend the definition so that the domain of u, v, w is not restricted to be non-negative but includes all integers. Such an extension constitutes a significant change of definition. We have defined a different function.

9.2.1 Function declarations

Pascal allows the programmer to define his own (non-standard) functions for use in a program. These definitions take the form of function declarations, which must follow variable declarations at the head of a block.

A function declaration itself consists of two parts, first the function heading, and then a block of program which computes the value to be returned by the function. The program heading incorporates the information about the function which we have just been discussing: the name of the function, the domain (that is, type) of each argument, and the codomain of the function, that is, the type of value returned by it. Thus the two *different* functions *diag* discussed above would have two different function headings as follows:

function $diag1\,(u, v, w : nonegint) : real;$
{Where *nonegint* has been previously defined by a type definition such as **type** $nonegint = 0..maxint;$}

function $diag2\,(u, v, w : integer) : real;$

To illustrate a complete function declaration, with both function heading
nd the block following it, we take a previously written program as an example.
he complete program *squareroot* which was given in Section 5.5.1 can be
written in the form of such a function declaration, as follows:

```
function squareroot (a, max : real) : real;
var old, new, relerr : real;
    begin
    old := (a + 1)/2;
        repeat
        new := (a/old + old)/2;
        relerr := abs((new − old)/(new + old));
        old := new
        until relerr < max;
    squareroot := new
    end; {of function squareroot}
```

The following points should be noted most carefully, since they are
ssential to all declarations of functions:

(i) The domain of each parameter is given by specifying its type, in the
example given:

$$(a, max : real)$$

(ii) After the parameter list comes another colon followed by a specification of the type of value returned by the function, that is, its
codomain, in this example it is again *real*.

(iii) Following the function heading comes a block which embodies declarations of local variables to be used within the statement part of the
function:

$$\text{var } old, new, relerr : real;$$

(iv) The statement part embodies the algorithm used to calculate the value
to be returned by the function. In order to indicate the value to be
returned it is essential to include an assignment statement, the left-
hand side of which is the function name, in this example:

$$squareroot := new$$

Once a function declaration has been made, the function may be used
nywhere in the program just as a standard function may be used.

9.3 PROCEDURES

Not all sub-programs are functions. In Pascal, those sub-programs which are no functions are called procedures, and the main distinquishing property is that a function always yields a resulting value whereas a procedure does not. Such a value may be a term in an expression, and so we can write expressions which include function-calls among their terms, for example:

$$x*y + a*sin(x) - c$$

but an expression cannot contain a procedure-call. We have met examples o procedures already, for example the standard procedures *read* and *write*, and it would clearly be nonsense to write an expression such as:

$$x*y + write(z)$$

because the function-call on the right does not yield a value which can be added to the term on the left.

We saw that there are standard functions and that a programmer is free to define his own functions. Similarly, a programmer is free to define his own procedures in addition to using those standard procedures provided by Pascal All such programmer-definitions must be embodied in the program in the form of procedure declarations.

9.3.1 Procedure declaration

Each procedure declaration has a similar form to that of a complete program except that:

   (i) The program heading is replaced by a procedure heading.

  (ii) The procedure heading is similar to a function heading except that of course, the specification of the type of value returned is omitted This is to be expected: a procedure does not return a value, so there is no codomain to be specified.

 (iii) The **end** which closes the block following a procedure (or function heading does *not* have a full stop after it.

It is worth noticing that a program, a function and a procedure are basically very similar in form. Each consists of a heading followed by a block. As procedures and functions have both been described as special forms of sub-programs this similarity in structure is both instructive and useful.

The problems and programs we have considered up until this point have been relatively simple, deliberately so, and as a result the program structure ha been so simple that sub-programs have not been required. In tackling less trivia problems, the approach described in Section 5.5 is inadequate. We shall introduce a broader based approach by a case-study of a slightly more complex problem That is, how to write a computer program to play noughts and crosses.

.4 CASE STUDY – NOUGHTS AND CROSSES
(also known as TICK-TACK-TOE)

'or simplicity we shall assume that *cross* always has first turn, and we shall
evise an algorithm to determine which square of the grid he should use at each
urn. Our first specification of a proposed algorithm is written in English, but
iven some of the trappings of a Pascal program:

> **program** *noughtsandcrosses(input, output)*;
>   **begin**
>   {move 1 ∗ ∗ ∗ ∗ ∗}
>   {go in a corner};
>   {move 2 ∗ ∗ ∗ ∗ ∗}
>   {if *nought* went in the middle then go in the opposite corner
>   otherwise go in a corner which is not adjacent to *nought* and is not
>   the opposite corner to *cross*};
>   {move 3 ∗ ∗ ∗ ∗ ∗}
>   {if there is a winning square for *cross*
>   then go in it
>   otherwise
>   if there is a winning square for *nought*
>   then go in that
>   otherwise go in a corner};
>   {subsequent moves ∗ ∗ ∗ ∗}
>   if there is a winning square for *cross*
>   then go in it
>   otherwise
>   if there is a winning square for *nought*
>   then go in it
>   otherwise go in any empty square}
>   **end**

This is our 'birds-eye view' of the algorithm. We now have three tasks:

(i) To satisfy ourselves of its correctness.

(ii) To choose data structures which are convenient for storing the information recording the state of the game as it progresses, and are also
convenient for carrying out the data processing required by the
algorithm.

(iii) To refine and expand the program by insertion of program fragments
following each comment, and by devising and writing sub-programs
which assist the process of refinement.

It cannot be too strongly emphasised that the first crude description of th algorithm is entirely independent of choice of data structures. This is essenti in order to achieve a clear specification of the basic meaning of our algorithm uncluttered by the kind of detail which arises from the way we choose to sto and manipulate the data. Furthermore, this form of specification is an importa part of the *documentation* of the program — that body of information require for understanding it, for assessing it, for ease of use by potential users, and f later modification, maintenance or improvement by any programmer, n necessarily the original author of the program.

This first specification serves as a blue-print which defines what th program is required to do. It should be suitable for giving to a programmer witho further information (except the rules of the game of noughts and crosses), a being sufficient to enable him to go away and write the required program, in a programming language, without ambiguity or misunderstanding.

Our choice of data structures should be conditioned by factors which v can select from a careful look at the program specification. A number of simp requirements seem to stand out:

  (i) Ease of identification of each square.

  (ii) Ease of identification of the row to which a square belongs.

  (iii) Ease of identification of the column to which a square belongs.

  (iv) Ease of identification of the squares belonging to each diagonal.

  (v) A simple convention for denoting the state of a square, that is wheth it is:

    (a) unused

    (b) occupied by a cross

    (c) occupied by a nought

A fairly obvious way of meeting these requirements is to represent the gr of squares by a two-dimensional array having three rows and three column each square being indexed by a pair of integers, the first denoting its row and th second its column. The value of each component may be conveniently chosen be a scaler type, say:

type *state* = (*blank, nought, cross*);

in which case our array for representing the grid in which the game is played w be:

var *square* : **array** [1..3, 1..3] **of** *state*;

and we shall initialise the state of the grid by a program fragment such as:

```
for row := 1 to 3 do
   for column := 1 to 3 do
      square [row, column] := blank;
```

Moves may easily be recorded in this scheme. If the move is for *cross*, and it is in, say, the centre square, then we can write:

    square [2, 2] := *cross*

For a corner square, it would be either:

    square [1, 1] := *cross*

or

    square [1, 3] := *cross*

or

    square [3, 1] := *cross*

or

    square [3, 3] := *cross*

Having made a trial choice of data structure, we are in a position to try using it in some refinement of our algorithm. We clearly need a sub-program which looks for a winning square, perhaps a function *win* whose parameter is either *nought* or *cross*, and which returns the row and column of the winning square as its value. This seems logically desirable, but unfortunately the design of the language Pascal imposes restrictions which do not allow it. The value returned by a Pascal function cannot be an array, though any scaler or sub-range type is allowed. All programming languages have limitations of one sort or another, and therefore whatever language one is using, it may happen at some time that one has to find a way round the limitations apparently imposed. One aspect of programming expertise is the imaginative development of the ability to find a way round such difficulties. Perhaps this may be compared with the expertise of an accountant, whose task is often to find legal ways of evading income tax. One solution to our current difficulty becomes plain when we remember that any multi-dimensional array may be mapped onto a one-dimensional array. Hence it is possible to map the pair of integers denoting row and column to a single integer, called *key*, using the relation:

    $key = 3*(row - 1) + column$

(note that there may be better ways of solving this problem which depend upon features of Pascal we have not yet introduced).

Next we tackle the problem of examining a given row to see if it contains a square which would make it a winning row. We should like a function which returns the integer value of the *key* to the winning square, using the value *nought* or *cross* as its actual parameter.

Working out the details of its body is tricky. We need to find a way to systematise the queries to be made of the squares 1, 2, and 3 in any row, such as:

    if 1 matches 2 then the other is? (3)
    if 2 matches 3 then the other is? (1)
    if 3 matches 1 then the other is? (2)

A little playing around with this table of values will lead to a convenient generalisation, that is, the identifying numbers 1, 2 and 3 always add up to 6. Hence
other is always numerically equal to the difference in value between 6 and the
sum of the numerical values of the two matching squares. The point is that we
want to find a matching pair of squares, that is, a pair of squares which both
contain say *cross*, and then we can test the other square to see if it contains
blank. If so then it is a winning square. One possible solution is given by the
following program fragment, which finds the winning square in a given row
and returns its *key* value, or returns zero if there is no winning square.

The declarations assumed are:

> **var** *compare, other, k* : *integer*;
>   *player* : *state*;

and the program fragment itself is:

```
key := 0;
   for k := 1 to 3 do
      begin
         compare := k mod 3 + 1;
         other := 6 − (k + compare);
         if square [row, k] = blank
         then
            if (square [row, other] = player)
            and
            (square [row, compare] = player)
            then
            key := 3*(row − 1) + k
   end;
```

This fragment can be expanded by inclusion in a **for** statement so that all three
rows are examined. It will then serve as the body of a function called, say,
winrow. A declaration for a similar function called *wincol* could be written as
follows:

```
function wincol (player : state) : integer;
var compare, other, k, row, col : integer
   begin
      wincol := 0;
         for col := 1 to 3 do
            for row := 1 to 3 do
               begin
                  compare := row mod 3 + 1;
                  other := 6 − (row + compare);
                  if square [row, col] = blank
                  then
```

```
                    if square [other, col] = player
                    and
                        square [compare, col] = player
                    then
                        wincol := 3*(row − 1) + col
          end
    end;
```

if the value returned by *wincol* is assigned to the integer variable *key*, then the index pair of the winning square can then be computed as follows:

$row := 1 + (key − 1)\textbf{div}3;$
$col := 1 + (key − 1)\textbf{mod}3$

Both the functions *winrow* and *wincol* can be written and tested by writing a test program whose purpose is simply to test them. It will then be realised that a *display* procedure is required which will print out the current state of the noughts and crosses grid at any time. A procedure to do this could therefore be written and tested. However, before any such activity is embarked upon, it is highly advisable to go back to the algorithm and try to rewrite it in expanded form, assuming the existence of the functions and procedures we have been discussing, in order to test whether these are convenient sub-programs to have.

```
begin
{move 1 for cross * * * *}
    square [1, 1] := cross; {or [1,3] or [3,1] or [3,3]]}
{move 2 for cross * * * *}
    if square [2, 2] = nought
    then square [3, 3] := cross
    else
        if square [1, 2] = blank
        then square [1, 3] := cross
        else square [3, 1] := cross;
{move 3 for cross * * * *}
{is there a winning row?}
key := winrow (cross);
    if key <> 0 {there is a winning square}
    then square [1 + (key − 1) div 3, 1 + (key − 1) mod 3] := cross
    {and the game is won}
    else {is there a winning column?}
      begin
        key := wincol(cross);
            if key <> 0 {there is a winning square}
            then
                square [1 + (key − 1) div 3, 1 + (key − 1) mod 3] := cross
                and the game is won
```

        else {is there a winning diagonal}
        begin
            key := *windiag*(*cross*);
            if *key* <> 0 {there is a winning square}
            then
                square [1 + (*key* − 1) **div** 3 + (*key* − 1) **mod** 3] := *cross*
                {and the game is won}
            else {can nought win? if so stop him}

At this point, it should be clear that the last comment must be replaced by a piece of program almost identical to the entire move 3 so far, with *cross* replaced by *nought* in all calls of the *winrow*, *wincol* and *windiag* functions. It would obviously be sensible to write a sub-program which corresponds to this complete process.

Another point which becomes clear at this point in the analysis is that the expressions for *key*, *row*, and *col* in terms of each other would be more simple if the row and column index for the array *square* each ran from 0 to 2 instead of from 1 to 3. Similarly, the values of *key* would need to run from 0 to 8 instead of from 1 to 9. The expressions then become:

$$row = key \text{ div } 3$$
$$col \ = key \text{ mod } 3$$
$$key = col + 3*row$$

Progressive refinement of an algorithm is facilitated by such mental inter-action between the birds-eye view approach and consideration of the basic units of program to be used as building blocks, that is, sub-programs. The birds-eye view approach is called top-down refinement, while consideration of the design of the basic units of sub-program is called bottom-up design. Conscious use of the see-saw between top-down and bottom-up techniques will be found to provide a cycle of progress in the process of designing a program which throws up design-faults quickly, rather than leaving their detection until a later stage when much effort has already been badly invested.

The purpose of this case study is not to arrive at a model solution of the problem posed, but rather to describe the journey and the preparations for the journey by means of which one may arrive at a solution. We shall therefore not complete this journey, but leave its solution for the list of problems at the end of the chapter. Before leaving it completely, however, a few words are called for on how to deal with *nought's* moves in the program. If the program is to be run at a keyboard terminal, it can be written to accept input via the keyboard, during the course of the game, by the user, who can input *nought's* moves. Otherwise, *nought's* moves must either be pre-planned and provided as data, or selected by the program, using a random number generator. This is not entirely satisfactory, but then *indirect* access to a computer never is!

9.5 A FUNCTION TO GENERATE RANDOM NUMBERS

A function which generates a sequence of pseudo-random numbers is often required, expecially when writing simulation programs, that is programs which simulate a physical system of some kind, the purpose of the random numbers being to simulate data to drive the program. A so-called pseudo-random number generator is a well-defined mathematical function, and obviously cannot generate random numbers, but there are many formuli, which can be used to generate a sequence of apparently random integer values in a given range, and this range can be mapped on to any other required range, such as 0 to 1. One of the commonly used methods is based upon residues (remainders) of integer division, using the formula:

$$X_{k+1} = (aX_k + c) \bmod m$$

Beginning with a starting value, X_0, each time the formula is used, a new X is generated. The operator **mod** gives the residue (that is, the remainder), when the operand on its left is divided by the operand on its right, both operands and the result being integers. In the formula given, a is known as the multiplier, c as the constant, and m as the modulus. The formula certainly does not generate pseudo-random numbers for all values of a, c and m, but it is fairly reliable provided the following rules of thumb are observed:

  (i) $m > X_0, m > a, m > c$
 (ii) a and m should be chosen so that they have no common factors.
(iii) Every prime factor of m is a factor of $(a - 1)$.
 (iv) If m is a multiple of 4, so is $(a - 1)$.
  (v) $a \leqslant 257$.

One suitable set of values is:

$$a = 5$$
$$c = 32719$$
$$m = 65437$$

EXAMPLE

Write a program which uses a function RAN(X) to generate a sequence of 300 random numbers between 0 and 1, and print them out, six on a line.

```
program RANDOMNUMBERS(output);
   const divi = 65436;
   var n, k, j : integer;
      val : real;
   function RAN(x : integer) : integer;
      const a = 5;
```

$$c = 32719;$$
$$m = 65437;$$

```
begin
    RAN := (a*x + c) mod m
end;
begin
    n := 1;
    for k := 1 to 50 do
        begin
            for j := 1 to 6 do
                begin
                    n := RAN(n);
                    val := n/divi;
                    write(val)
                end;
            writeln
        end
end.
```

9.6 PROBLEMS

9.6.1

Write a function $tan(x)$, taking care to ensure tnat a program using this function will not abort for sensitive values of x. Test the program, providing sensitive values and check the accuracy obtained by your function, particularly for very large values of x.

9.6.2

Complete the analysis of the noughts and crosses simulation, and write the program to play it, using a random number generator to produce nought' moves.

9.6.3

Design, and develop and write a procedure to make nought's moves. Insert this in the program produced for Section 9.6.2, in place of the random number generator. Use the random number generator to make the first move for cross.

CHAPTER 10

Lines of communications

'I sent a message to the fish
I told them this is what I wish.
The little fishes of the sea
They sent a message back to me.

Lewis Carroll

10.1 COMMUNICATION WITH VARIABLES

10.1.1 Block structure and the scope of names

A Pascal program consists of a program heading followed by a single block. A block is a number of declarations followed by a compound statement. Both functions and procedures in Pascal have a similar structure, that is, a heading followed by a single block. Again, the block is a number of declarations followed by a compound statement. Now function and procedure declarations may be found among those at the start of any block, whether it is the main program block, or a block contained within a function or procedure declaration. In all cases, a block is a compact single entity, and it is important to understand the relation between the declarations in a block on the one hand, and its compound statement on the other. The essence of this relation is as follows:

(i) The storage space required for the declarations is made available whenever the flow of program control enters the block to which the declarations belong. The same storage space is discarded and becomes unavailable whenever program control exits from the block.

(ii) The names used in the declarations are effective only within the block to which they belong. Clearly they cannot be so outside the block because the storage space to which they refer does not exist.

Thus in any part of a Pascal program, a quantity, function or procedure represented by a particular indentifer may be either *existent* or *non-existent*. For example, in the program RANDOMNUMBERS (Section 9.5), the quantities whose identifers are *divi*, *n*, *k*, and *j* exist all the time the program is running, whereas the quantities whose identifiers are *a*, *c*, and *m* come into existence each time the function *RAN* is entered, and cease to exist each time exit from it occurs. If, for instance, we inserted immediately before the final **end** of the program:

write (*a*, *c*, *m*)

the program would fail to compile and the compiler would issue an error message stating that *a*, *c*, and *m* had not been declared, and this is correct because they have not been declared in the main program block, only within the function block.

If, instead, we inserted immediately before the **end** of the function block:

write (*k*)

this would be perfectly legal. The variable *k* is declared in the main block. The function block is part of this block, and therefore this reference to *k* would be within the *scope* of its declaration.

It is possible for a quantity to be existent but inaccessable. This happens if the same identifier is chosen for two declarations, one in an enclosing block, the other within an inner block.

EXAMPLE OF INACCESSABILITY

> **program** *SCOPES* (*output*);
> **var** *A*, *B*, *C*, *D* : *integer*;
> **procedure** *innerblock*;
>   **var** *x*, *y*, *z*, *D* : *real*;
>   **begin** {in this compound statement, the integer variables *A*, *B*, *C* are existent and accessable. The *integer* variable *D* is existent but inaccessible: it has been masked by the declaration of the *real* variable *D*. The *real* variables *x*, *y*, *z*, *D* are existent and accessable.}
>   *x* := 10;
>   *y* := 20;
>   *z* := 30;
>   *D* := 40;
>   *writeln* (*x*, *y*, *z*, *D*, ', inside innerblock')
>   **end**;
> **begin** {in this compound statement, the integer variables *A*, *B*, *C*, *D* are all existent and accessable. The real variables *x*, *y*, *z*, *D* are non-existent.}
>   *A* := 1;
>   *B* := 2;
>   *C* := 3;
>   *D* := 4;
>   *innerblock*;
>   *writeln* (*D*)
> **end**.

QUESTION: What value is printed when the last statement in the program, *writeln(D)*, is executed? Is it 4 or 40? After all the last three statements are:

> *D* := 4;
> *innerblock*;
> *writeln(D)*

The first one assigns the value 4 to *D*. The second activates the procedure *innerblock*, inside which there is a statement:

> *D* := 40

The third statement is *writeln(D)*.

ANSWER: There are two completely different variables called *D*. Within *innerblock*, the *integer D* declared in main program block is existent but inaccessible, because it is masked by the declaration of *real D*. Hence the assignment of the value 40 is to *real D*, but the value of *integer D* remains unchanged as 4. The *writeln(D)* statement occurs in the outer block where *real D* does not exist, and it naturally writes the value of *integer D* which does exist and has the value, 4.

0.1.2 What use is block structure?

The scope rules of block structure which have just been described facilitate the step by step refinement of a program into self-contained modules. When a very large program is being developed by a team of programmers, each programmer may be delegated the task of writing one or more procedures or functions, and there is no danger of interaction between these modules arising through the accidental choice of identical names for local working variables in separate modules.

A procedure or function may be designed, developed, written and tested, quite idependently of other procedures and functions. This means that programs may be designed top-down, but written and tested bottom-up. This approach means that errors are localised and easier to remedy. As each procedure or function is finished and tested, it may be incorporated into the developing program which is used to test the proper functioning of all the modules, as they are added, one by one, to the program.

It is good programming style to declare variables in the smallest block within which they are required. If they are declared in an outer block, they may be referenced, and their values changed within any of the procedures or functions declared within that block. Such changes are half-hidden from the reader of the main program, and instead of the modules being independent, they interact with each other, with the result that two procedures may appear to execute correctly when each is tested separately, but, because of interaction, they fail to do so when they are both incorporated into the program. In any case, the overall effect is obscure to say the least, as may be seen by trying to work out what output is produced by the following program:

```
program sideeffects;
var J, K, L : integer;
procedure sillyone;
   begin
      J := J − 1;
      K := K + 1;
      L := 2*L
   end;
procedure swap;
var temp : integer;
   begin
      temp := J;
      J := K;
      K := temp
   end;
begin
   J := 1;
   K := 2;
   L := 3;
   sillyone;
   swap;
   sillyone;
   swap;
   sillyone;
   writeln(' J =', J, ', K =', K, ', L =', L)
end.
```

10.2 COMMUNICATION WITH SUB-PROGRAMS

10.2.1 Value parameters − call by value

We have already seen that procedures and functions can gain access to the data of an enclosing block in two ways:

(i) by operations on non-local variables, that is, variables declared in the enclosing outer block;

(ii) by values being passed from the outer block via parameters.

The following program finds the square root of a real positive value to within a given maximum relative error, following the same method as was used in Section 5.5.1, but making use of a function $root(x)$:

```
program squareroot(input, output);
var a, max : real;
function root(X : real) : real;
   var old, new, relerr : real;
   begin
      old := (x + 1)/2;
      repeat
         new := (x/old + old)/2;
         relerr := abs((new − old)/(new + old));
         old := new
      until relerr < max;
      root := new
   end;
begin
   read(a, max);
   writeln(a, max);
   writeln(root(a))
end.
```

There are three lines of communication here between the main program and the function, two passing information to the function, the other passing back information to the main program:

(i) The global variable *max*, declared in the main program block, is used inside the function.

(ii) The value of the global variable *a*, declared in the main program block, is passed as an actual parameter to the function *root*, and this is the value substituted for the formal parameter x on entry to root.

(iii) The result value yielded by the function is passed back to the main program, when the function has been evaluated, and it becomes the actual parameter to the procedure *write*, when that is called.

In the function $root(x)$, x is said to be a formal parameter called by value. This means that when the function is entered, the formal parameter is assigned the value of the actual parameter used in the call.

In general, the actual parameter used in the case of a call by value is an expression. In the example given, the expression was, simply, *a*. However, it is equally possible to use more complicated expressions. We could write:

$root(2*a − 1)$
$root(a + cos(a) − 3)$
$root(3.14159)$
$root(maxint − 1)$

In each case, the value of the expression is computed and, on entry to the function, it is assigned to the formal parameter.

10.2.2 Address parameters – call by name

Sometimes we want a sub-program to pass back more than one piece of information to the main program. For example, the program *maxandpos* in Section 7.4.1 found the maximum value in an array and its position, or subscript. If we tried to turn this program into a sub-program we should need to return two results which are mathematically independent.

To do this, we can write a procedure which uses *variable parameters* as distinct from *value* parameters. This means that the actual parameter passed is not a value but in machine terms, an address, that is, the address in store of a variable. In Pascal we do not deal actually with *addresses* – we *refer* to them by symbolic *names*. This kind of parameter passing is therefore described alternatively as call by *name*, call by *reference*, or call by *address*.

When call by name is required, this must be specified in the procedure heading by indicating that the parameter concerned is a variable, not a value expression. When a parameter is called by name, the actual parameter must be a variable name, not an expression, and the information passed to the sub-program is the address of the variable, not merely its value. This means that the value of the variable can be changed within the sub-program because, its address being known (by the system), it is possible to assign values to the variable.

EXAMPLE

Write a function *found* which returns a boolean value *true* if it finds a particular value in an array A of 20 *char* values, and also passes back, by means of a variable parameter, the subscript of the array element where the value was found. If the value is not found, the function return value must be *false*:

```
function found (item : char, var subscript : integer) : boolean;
   begin
      subscript := 0;
      repeat
         subscript := subscript + 1
      until (A [subscript] = item) or (subscript = 20);
      found := (A [subscript] = item)
   end
```

This example uses all four of the possible means of communication between program and sub-program:

(i) return of value yielded by function evaluation;
(ii) return of value by variable parameter called by name;
(iii) passing of value by value parameter called by value;
(iv) passing of value by reference to global variable from within the sub-program.

A more detailed treatment of call by name and call by value is given in Chapter 15.

3 COMMUNICATION WITH PROGRAM BRANCHLINES – THE CASE STATEMENT

gram flow of control sometimes reaches a branch point. One of the program
.trol structures for dealing with a branch point is the **if, then, else** statement,
ch was described in Section 4.5, conditional statements. This structure is
igned for use when there is a choice between two alternatives. It can be
pted when there are more than two, but becomes unwieldly, and the resulting
gram lacks both clarity and efficiency.

:AMPLE

ite a program fragment to print out the strings $'one'$, $'two'$, $'three'$, $'four'$,
her', accordingly as the value of the integer variable k is 1, 2, 3, 4 or something
e:

```
if (k < 1) or (k > 4)
then write('other')
else
   if k < 3
   then
     if k = 1
     then write('one')
     else write('two')
   else
     if k = 3
     then write('three')
     else write('four')
```

It may be easily imagined that the result would be even worse if there were
pre than five possibilities of interest. Pascal provides a control structure called
: **case** statement, which is designed to deal with this situation. Using it, we can
vrite the preceding program fragment as follows:

```
if (k < 1) or (k > 4)
then write('other')
else
   case k of
     1 : write('one');
     2 : write('two');
     3 : write('three');
     4 : write('four')
   end
```

The syntactic form of the case statement is:

'case' expression 'of'
   case-label-list ':' statement;
      ● ● ●
   case-label-list ':' statement
'end'

The case-label-list is a list of one or more scalar constants which act
alternative labels to each statement. Each labels list is separated from its sta
ment by a colon. The value of the expression following **case** must also be scal
and it is used as a selector, selecting for execution that statement having a lab
whose value is equal to that of the selector. Upon completion of the select
statement, control goes to the **end** of the **case** statement. The actual order
the labels, or of the labels lists is immaterial − it is the scalar value of each lab
which determines its selection.

If there is no label whose value is equal to the current value of the select
expression, the effect is undefined. This is effectively a programming error. Noti
that this possibility was eliminated in the example given, by the use of the co
ditional statement preceding the case statement. It is good programming practi
always to ensure that the selector expression cannot select a non-existent lab
by using such a test. An example of a case statement with labels lists follows:

if $(ch < 'a')$ **or** $(ch > 'z')$
then *symbol* := *notletter*
else
  case *ch* **of**
    $'a', 'e', 'i', 'o', 'u'$: *symbol* := *vowel*;
    $'b', 'c', 'd', 'f', 'g',$
    $'h', 'j', 'k', 'l', 'm',$
    $'n', 'p', 'q', 'r', 's',$
    $'t', 'v', 'w', 'x', 'y',$
    $'z'$: *symbol* := *consonant*
  end

Note that this program fragment works correctly only on computers whi
use an internal character code whose values for letters occur in an unbrok
sequence. This is true in the ASCII code, but not in EBCDIC. The ordering
the EBCDIC code is such that some characters which are not letters occur
various groups between the code for $'a'$ and the code for $'z'$. Hence the te
preceding the above **case** statement fails to *ensure* that the case selector val
be always one which corresponds to one of the case labels, when EBCDIC co
is in use.

10.4 PROBLEMS

10.4.1

Write a function which returns the value of *epsilon*, using the algorithm described in Section 2.3.3.

10.4.2

Write a procedure *hexout*(*int* : *integer*) which writes a hexadecimal string corresponding to the value of *int*.

10.4.3

Write a procedure *octalout*(*int* : *integer*) which writes an octal representation of the value of *int*.

10.4.4

Write the following procedures:

(i) *matread* to read in a three-by-three real matrix.
(ii) *matwrite* to write out a three-by-three real matrix.
(iii) *matprod* to multiply two three-by-three matrices together and give the product matrix.

10.4.5

Using the procedures of Section 10.4.4, write a program to read in pairs of matrices and print them out together with their product.

10.4.6

Write a program which will read in an integer value, say *n*, followed by *n* integer values, print out all the values and then print out the middle value. If *n* is even it should print out the two middle values.

CHAPTER 11

Data-processing with sequential files

'What sort of things do you remember best?', Alice ventured to ask. 'Oh, things that happen the week after next,' the Queen replied in a careless tone. 'For instance, now, there's the King's messenger. He's in prison now, being punished: and the trial doesn't even begin till next Wednesday and of course the crime comes last of all.' 'Suppose he never commits the crime?' said Alice. 'That would be all the better, wouldn't it?' the Queen said.

Lewis Carroll

11.1 ON YOUR MARK, GET SET . . .

Every sequential file has a beginning, and before one may start processing with a file, whether reading or writing, just as with a book, one must open it at the beginning. Pascal does this automatically for the two standard files *input* and *output*, but all other files used by the programmer must be opened at the beginning either:

or

    (a) for reading, by using *reset*,

    (b) for writing, by using *rewrite*.

for example:

    reset(*f*);
    reset(*g*);
    rewrite(*h*);
      • • •

Every non-standard file used in a Pascal program must be declared in the program, and, if it exists externally to the program, it must be passed as a parameter in the program heading. We have already seen that the standard files *input* and *output* are passed as parameters in the program heading in this way. Files are the only type of parameter allowed in the program heading.

It is worth noting at this point that although the program heading is very similar in appearance to a procedure heading, there are some important differences, both in appearance and meaning. In a program heading:

    (i) The type of a parameter is not specified. This is because only type **file** is allowed.

    (ii) Although file parameters are, obviously, always called by name, and not by value, this is not specified either.

In waiving the need for specification of type, and name-call, and assuming them by default, Pascal makes the program heading shorter and less cumbersome, but the underlying semantics should not be overlooked, even though they are implied rather than explicit.

11.2 END OF FILE

We have already met the technique of reading in a value which tells the program how many data values there are to follow. The snag about this is that we do not always know how many, and in any case, we may not have written the datafile. However, the computing system can detect when it has reached the end of the file it is reading, and this information can be made available within a Pascal program by means of the standard function *eof*, whose identifier is built from the initial letters of 'end of file'. The function *eof* yields a boolean result *true* or *false*, *true* if the 'next item to be read' is beyond the end of file, and *false* otherwise.

EXAMPLE

Write a program to count the number of values in an *input* file of *integers*:

```
program intcount (input, output);
var count, x : integer;
  begin
    count := 0;
  if not eof then read (x);
  while not eof do
        begin
          count := count + 1;
          read (x)
        end;
    writeln (' count = ', count)
  end.
```

The most general use of the function *eof* is to enable a program to process all the data in a file, regardless of the exact number of items of data, without the need for special markers, and without modifications to the program being needed for different quantities of data.

When the file being read is not *input*, *eof* takes as a parameter the identifer of the file being read, for example, *eof (gertrude)*, where gertrude is the name of the file.

11.3 FILE TYPES

Like arrays, files are structured variables. In Pascal, every **file** is a sequential file: it is a sequence of components all of which are themselves the same type. The

quential attribute is implied in every declaration of a **file**, but the declaration
ust be explicit about the type of the file's components. We may choose to
fine a file-type, and this will have the form:

type $F =$ **file of** T;

ere T is the type of all the components of files of type F. For example, there
a standard type, *text*, whose definition is:

type *text* $=$ **file of** *char*;

d this makes possible the declaration of files of type text as follows. For
ample:

var *gertrude, millicent, augustus* : *text*;

ternatively, we could choose to combine the last two declarations by the
uivalent single declaration:

var *gertrude, millicent, augustus* : **file of** *char*;

Sequential files are an important part of any serious computer system. One
ason alone which makes them indispensable is that there is always some finite
nit to the size of the main store. Main store is that part of store which can be
cessed quickly and randomly. It is usually more expensive than secondary
ore, but in addition there may be a physical limit to its size imposed by the
chitecture of the computing system, for example the number of different
umerical) machine addresses which can be represented in some arbitrary but
edetermined number of bits — the *size* of an *address*. Secondary store can
nsist of many different kinds of physical devices which will provide means of
ansferring data between main, random-access store and sequential files.

The devices in common use include:

   (i) Disks.
  (ii) Magnetic tapes.
 (iii) Cardreaders and papertape readers.
 (iv) Cardpunches and papertapepunches.
  (v) Line-printers.

A sequential file may be thought of as a generalised abstraction of all
vices of this kind. Some of the devices differ from others. For example, discs
d magnetic tapes may be repositioned, whereas punches and line-printers
nnot be repositioned. However, it is useful to think of a sequential file (possibly
ored on disk) which is destined for output on a punch, as a punch file, or of a
le destined to be printed on a line-printer as a line-printer file. The generali-
tion of all in the concept of sequential files makes possible the definition of a
neral operation of inspection of a sequential file.

11.4 BUFFERS

To fix our ideas, we shall consider input of *text* files, that is, **file of** *char*. At a
given moment, with such a file, the only data accessible is the *next char*. W
might think of the sequence of chars as being represented on a sequence
frames on a celluloid ribbon of film. At any moment, one and only one particu.
frame is projected on to the viewing screen. The viewing screen fulfills the r
of a buffer variable whose contents are, always, the next char to be read. T
word 'buffer' is commonly used as a technical computing term to signify
temporary storage location for a piece of data in transit. If large quantities
data are to be transferred from *A* to *B*, each piece comes from a different locati
in *A* and goes to a different location in *B*. It is usual to simplify this operati
into two steps — the first step transfers one piece at a time from the differe
location in *A* to a buffer — the second step transfers from the buffer to t.
different location in *B*.

Every Pascal file automatically has a buffer-variable, and this is denoted
appending the character '↑' to the file identifier. Thus the buffer variable for t
file *f* is *f↑*, and for *gertrude* is *gertrude↑*. The value (that is, contents) of a buff
variable may be assigned to an ordinary variable of corresponding type in t
normal way.

For example, if *x*, *y*, and *z* are of type *char*, we may write:

> *x* := *gertrude↑*;
> *y* := *gertrude↑*;
> *z* := *gertrude↑*;

then *x*, *y*, and *z* will all have the same value as *gertrude↑*.

11.5 THE PROCEDURE *get*

The only way of changing the value of the buffer variable of a file being read,
to advance the file by one *char*. This is like advancing our celluloid film by o
frame, with the result that a new frame is projected onto the viewing scree
If we write:

> *get*(*gertrude*)

the effect is to assign to *gertrude↑* the value of the next *char* in *gertrude*.

The effect of the two consecutive statements:

> *x* := *gertrude↑*;
> *get*(*gertrude*);

is exactly equivalent to the single statement:

> *read*(*gertrude*, *x*);

Notice the order of the former two statements. Immediately after a statement:

reset(gertrude)

the buffer variable *gertrude*↑ contains the value of the very first *char* in the **file** *gertrude*. In other words, immediately after a *reset*, we are looking at the first frame. Assigning the value of the buffer variable to *x* does not change the *positioning* of the file. The only way to do this is to use *get*.

If *gertrude*↑ contains the very last *char* of the file *gertrude*, then the effect of performing:

get(gertrude)

is to move the file past its end-of-file mark, and the value of *gertrude*↑ becomes undefined. In addition, the value of *eof(gertrude)* becomes *true*.

11.6 THE PROCEDURE *put*

In addition to reading a sequential file, we may wish to write one. In this case the situation is a kind of inverse or mirror image of the reading situation. Suppose we wish to write a **file** of *char* called *daisy*. The first thing to do is to position the file at its beginning. To do this we need the statement:

rewrite(daisy)

At this point, the buffer variable *daisy*↑ has not been initialised and is therefore undefined. Since we are writing, not reading, the buffer variable is no longer a projection of the next frame in the file. Instead, it is now more comparable to the viewfinder of a camera. In order to 'write' on our film, first we must point the view finder at the required data, say:

daisy↑ := *x*;

and secondly, we must press the button which exposes the film to the view in the viewfinder window:

put(daisy);

This copies the contents of the buffer variable *daisy*↑ onto the file daisy and advances the file to the next position. Thus the two consecutive statements:

daisy↑ := *x*;
put(daisy);

are exactly equivalent to:

write(daisy, x);

After *rewrite(daisy)*, *eof(daisy)* becomes *true*. After *put(daisy)*, *eof(daisy)* remains *true* and *daisy*↑ becomes undefined (Pascal Report 10.1.1).

11.7 MERGING SEQUENTIAL FILES

A common computing application is the sorting of data, and it frequently happens that two files, say f and g each contain sorted data (say integers), and it is desired to combine the two files into one in such a way that the contents of the new file, say h, are sorted.

A simple method of doing this is called *merging* the two files f and g. The method is to compare the pair of next values on f and g. Whichever is less is copied to h, and the file from which it came is advanced one position. This process is repeated until one of the files is empty (that is, *eof* is *true*). Then the remaining contents of the other file copied to h, for example:

```
program merge (f, g, h);
{f, g, h are external files of integers}
var f, g, h : file of integer;
  begin
     reset (f);
     reset (g);
     rewrite (h);
       while not (eof (f) or eof (g)) do
         begin
           if f↑ < g↑
           then
               begin
                 h↑ := f↑;
                 get (f)
               end
           else
               begin
                 h↑ := g↑;
                 get (g)
               end;
           put (h)
         end;
       while not eof (f) do
         begin
           h↑ := f↑;
           put (h);
           get (f)
         end;
       while not eof (g) do
         begin
           h↑ := g↑;
           put (h);
           get (g)
         end
  end.
```

11.8 INPUT/OUTPUT FINE CONTROL

11.8.1 Line-printer paper-feed control characters

The text is usually structured by being divided into lines, and the physical design of very many line-printers takes account of this fact by interpreting the first character of each line sent to it as a paper-feed control code. Although not a national or international standard, there is a widespread convention which treats each character as follows, when it occurs as first character in the line:

'+'   no paper-feed (the previous line is overprinted)
blank   paper-feed single-line spacing
'0'   paper-feed double-line spacing
'1'   paper-feed to top of next page

any other character causes paper-feed single-line spacing.

These conventions may be exploited independently of the programming language being used. They are a feature of line-printers, not of Pascal. When using character output, they give fine control over some aspects of the printed output. In particular:

(i)   Output of composite characters may be achieved by overprinting, for example the Greek letter 'ϕ' may be achieved by overprinting 'o' and '/'.

(ii) A particular case of overprinting is the case of underlining by overprint of the underline character.

(iii) By overprinting the same line twice, that is, printing the line three times with no line feed in between, **bold** print may be achieved.

(iv) As previously mentioned, double-line spacing, and page throw are possible.

Notice that the control character is not of course printed. If a file is sent to the line-printer and control characters have been omitted, the line-printer will still interpret the first character of each line as a control character, so this character will not be printed. Furthermore, there will be 'mysterious' effects when it happens by chance to be '+', '0', or '1'.

Because of this feature, special care is required when writing strings at the beginning of a line, always to start the string with a space. When writing numeric values, the system takes care of this automatically.

11.8.2 End-of-line, standard functions — *eoln* and *readln*

The Pascal standard function *eoln* operates in a similar way with regard to an end of line as does the *eof* function with regard to an end of file. By default, it refers to the standard file *input*, but it may be given a parameter which is a filename, for example *eoln*(*millicent*) in which case it refers to the file of that name. It returns the boolean value *true* if *millicent*↑ corresponds to the position of a line separator, in which case the value of millicent↑ is the blank character, otherwise the value of *eoln* is *false*.

The function is useful in reading squential files whose contents are structured into lines, when it is desirable to carry out some processing a line at a time. This may be so either for text or for files of fixed length records such as card-images.

EXAMPLE

```
program processlines (input, output);
var col : integer;
    buffer : array [1..100] of char;
  begin
    while not eof do
      begin
        col := 0;
          while not eoln do
            begin
              col := col + 1;
              read (buffer [col])
            end;
          readln;
          for k := col + 1 to 100 do
            buffer [col] := ' ';
          {process data in current line held in buffer}
                  • • •
      end
  end.
```

The comment {process data in current line held in buffer} is of course to be followed by a program fragment which carries out the processing required.

The standard procedure *readln* may be used either without parameters, or with the same parameters as *read*, and its behaviour may be described in two stages. If *readln* is used with parameters, then the first stage of behaviour is equivalent to *read*. If there are no parameters, then the first stage does nothing at all. The second stage behaviour of *readln* is to skip the remainder of the current line, past end-of-line, so that the file buffer is advanced to the start of the next line, after which *eoln*, if tested, returns the value *false*. Thus, if *f* is a file, *readln(f)* is equivalent to the two consecutive statements:

while not *eoln(f)* **do** *get(f)*;
get(f);

The first statement skips to end-of-line, when *eoln* becomes *true*. The second moves the file buffer past end-of-line, so that *eoln* becomes *false*.

If *readln* were not included in the program *processlines*, the program would
ever get beyond the end of the first line of input data. The value of *eoln*
ould remain *true*, and the program would find itself in an endless loop, testing
of and *eoln*.

1.8.3 The standard procedures *write* and *writeln*

he full facilities of *write* and *writeln* give very fine control over layout of
utput. Both procedures have the same general syntactic notational form:

write (*filename*, p1, p2, ..., pn)
writeln (*filename*, p1, p2, ..., pn)

here the *filename* must be included unless it is *output*, when it may be omitted
nd is assumed by default.
Each of the p parameters may take any of the forms:

   (i) value
  (ii) value ':' min-field-width
 (iii) value ':' min-field-width ':' fraction length

alue   may be an expression of type *char*, *integer*, *real*, *boolean* or a
                    string.

in-field-width   must be an expression of type *integer*. It indicates the minimum
                    number of positions to be used in printing value, preceding
                    blanks being inserted if necessary. If this space is too small for
                    the value supplied, then more space will be used.

                    A *real* value must be written with at least one preceding
                    blank.

                    If min-field-width is omitted, a default value is assumed
                    by the system, suitable to the type of the value being printed.

action-length   must be of type *integer*. It is meaningful *only* if the value to
                    be printed is of type *real*, and specifies the number of digits
                    to follow the decimal point. When it is used, the value is
                    printed in fixed-point representation; if omitted then floating-
                    point representation is used by default (see Section 2.1.1).

XAMPLES

   (i) *write*(18.63215 : 8 : 3) will print

        18.632

        preceded by two blanks.
  (ii) *write*(18.63215) will print

        1.86321500E+001

        (making some arbitrary assumptions about installation-dependent
        defaults.)

11.9 PROBLEMS

11.9.1

Given an external file of text called *data*, write a program to copy the content to the *output* file, leaving a margin of 5 blanks on the left of each line, and using double-line spacing.

11.9.2

Write a program which reads in the day of the week of 1st January and the year and prints out a calendar for the year, printing 1 month on each page.

11.9.3

Write a procedure which enables the output of a string of up to seven characters in 'banner headline' style, each character output taking a matrix of up to 12 X 12 print positions (that is, 12 cols and 12 rows). Include only the letters of your surname (or part of it). Write a program which calls the procedure.

11.9.4

Choose a full-page black and white illustration from a magazine. Rule lines across the picture at equal intervals both vertically and horizontally, dividing into a matrix of 40 X 40.

    Assign a digit between 0 and 4 to each box denoting its intensity (0 = white ..., 4 = black). Write a program to read a representation of it, using composite characters (overprinted) to obtain the various intensities: white, feint, grey, dark black.

11.9.5

Write a program called *double* which reads in a text file from *input* and prints its contents in two columns side by side, so that each line printer page contains two columns or 'pages' of text, each having 50 characters per line and 50 lines per page.

CHAPTER 12

Data structures

'All knitting stiches are based on just two methods – knitting and purling – and however complicated patterns may appear they are all achieved by simple, or intricate arrangements of these two methods to produce an almost infinite variety of fabric and texture.'

Pam Dawson

12.1 RECORDS

Everyone is familiar with the idea of a *record*, a collection of attributes relating to some particular entity, for example, a student's record of name, home-address, birthdate, sex, enrolment date, course, etc., a stock record for each item of stock held by a business, or the catalogue record for each book in a library. The essential feature of a record is that its components may be quite different from each other in kind.

In Pascal there is a specially provided data structure for a record, with a fixed number of components called fields. A type definition is used to specify the field identifier for each component and its type. Any number of components may be specified in this way. Type definitions may be followed by variable declarations in the usual way.

EXAMPLES

```
type date = record
              year : integer;
              month : 1..12;
              day : 1..31
            end;

type bookrecord = record
                    title : packed array [1..39] of char;
                    author : packed array [1..12] of char;
                    publisher : packed array [1..24] of char;
                    classification : packed array [1..8] of char;
                    cataloguenum : integer;
                    entrydate : date
                  end;

var book : array [1..maxint] of bookrecord;
    today, yearend, duedate : date;
```

Notice that the variable declaration just made declares an array of records. The following program fragment will assign values to one entire record, and illustrates how field selectors may be used to identify particular fields, a point being used to separate fieldname from recordname:

```
today.year := 1980;
today.month := 12;
today.day := 31;
```

This is a little clumsy, and Pascal makes provision for a more convenient notation achieving exactly the same result as the foregoing example by using the **with** statement:

```
with today do
begin
  year := 1980;
  month := 12;
  day := 31
end
```

A Pascal record is very flexible. Any field of a record may itself be of any type which has been defined. It may itself be a record, or an array, or even an array of records. Since records may be nested within records, **with** statements may be correspondlingly nested.

The value of an entire record may be assigned quite simply, for example:

```
yearend := today;
```

To initialise the record for a book in the catalogue we could use the following program fragment:

```
with book [1001] do
  begin
    title := 'Foundations of Programming, with Pascal';
    author := 'Lawrie Moore';
    publisher := 'Ellis Horwood Limited    ';
    classification := 'superb  ';
    cataloguenum := 1001;
    entrydate := today
  end;
```

On adding a second volume in response to demand, the required entries would be, say:

```
book [1053] := book [1001] ;
book [1053] .entrydate := today;
```

(It is assumed that, in the meantime, the value of *today* has been updated).

Note that all the strings must have the correct length in order to conform
the types specified in the type definition of *bookrecord*. Strings of different
ngth are of different type. Correct length is achieved by padding out with
ailing blanks.

2.1.1 A record with a variant field

ascal allows the final field of any record to be of variant type. This is done by
ie use of a case statement, within the record type definition, providing alter-
ative field types for different cases. To continue the illustration of records
ept for a library, we might have a record of bookstatus for each book, which
cords whether the book is in the library and available for loan, or is out on
an, in which case the membership number of the borrower, and the due date
return are recorded, for example:

```
type bookstat = (free, lent),
type bookstatus =    record
                        cataloguenum : integer;
                          case bs : bookstat of
                              free : (classification : array [1..8] of char);
                              lent : (borrower : integer; duedate : date)
                          end {of case}
                      end {of record};
```

2.1.2 The syntax of record definitions

```
record-type = 'record' field-list 'end';
field-list = fixed-part | fixed-part ';' variant-part | variant-part;
fixed-part = record-section ';' record-section ;
record-section = field-identifier ',' field-identifier ':' type | empty;
```

ie syntax of the variant part is:

```
variant-part = 'case' tag-field type-identifier 'of' variant ';' variant;
variant = case-label-list ';' field-list | empty;
tag-field = identifier ':' | empty;
```

2.2 SETS OF BITS
2.2.1 What is a set?

'e have already seen, in Chapter 2, that the set of bits which constitute a *word*
computer store may be used to represent data in many different ways. If we
gard them simply as boolean atoms, they provide an extremely useful physical
odel of the mathematical concept of a set.

In the case of small set, by far the most simple and unambiguous way ƍ defining a particular set is by giving a list of the elements which constitute i entire membership.

Pascal provides a data structure which allows manipulation with sets, but imposes strong restrictions which enable Pascal sets to be represented an modelled by bitstrings of fixed length. The main restrictions are:

(i) The members of a set must be of the same type.

(ii) The only types allowed are those which have absolutely precise value that is, *boolean, char, scalar, subrange*, or *integer*.

(iii) The maximum size of set is limited because it is machine-dependen In practice it is limited to the number of bits in a *word* of comput memory.

The set operations provided in Pascal are the fundamental mathematical s operations. There are three tests, one to test whether a given element is a memb of a set, and the second to test whether all members of one set are members ƍ another. The first test is called membership and the second inclusion. The thir test is for equality between two sets, which means they have exactly the sam membership. The membership of element e in set x is expressed in Pascal ι (e **in** x). The inclusion of set x in set y in Pascal is expressed as ($x < y$). Th equality of two sets u and v is expressed in Pascal by ($u = v$). All three of th foregoing expressions are *boolean* expressions.

In addition to the tests, there are three operations, each of which forms new set from two existing sets. These are set union, set intersection, and s difference. These will be explained.

(a) **Set union**

The union of two sets is the set whose members are members of eith or both the original sets. For example, if the set A = [3, 17, −1, 4] an the set B = [29, 3, 4, 18, 155] the set C which is the union of A and (written as C := A + B in Pascal) is the set C = [3, 17, −1, 4, 29, 1 155].

(b) **Set intersection**

The intersection of two sets is the set whose members are members ' common of both the original sets. For example, the set D formed t intersection of A and B, in Pascal

D := A*B

consists of the set

D = [3, 4]

(c) **Set difference**

The difference between two sets A and B is the set E whose members belong to A but not B. In Pascal

$$E := A - B$$

consists of the set

$$E = [17, -1]$$

2.2.2 Correspondence between set operations, and logical operations

we use the bitstring as our model of set representation, we may think of each it as a boolean variable. For example, consider the set of the three colours [red, hite, blue], and suppose we have variables w, x, y, and z, each of which is e name of a set, and whose values are:

$x = [red, white, blue]$
$y = [white]$
$z = [red, whi\ blue]$
$w = [\quad]$ {the empty set}

he bitstring representations of these values are:

$x = 1\ 1\ 1$
$y = 0\ 1\ 0$
$z = 1\ 0\ 1$
$w = 0\ 0\ 0$

he operation of union between say y and z is represented by carrying out the gical **or** operation between corresponding bits of y and z:

$$y + z = 1\ 1\ 1$$

he operation of intersection between say x and z is represented by carrying out e logical **and** operation between corresponding bits of x and z:

$$x * z = 1\ 0\ 1$$

he operation of set difference between say x and z is represented by carrying ut the logical operation **and not** between corresponding bits of x and z:

$$x - z = 0\ 1\ 0$$

ther examples:

$x * w = 0\ 0\ 0$
$y - w = 0\ 1\ 0$
$y * z = 0\ 0\ 0$

12.2.3 Venn diagrams

Suppose we have three sets of girls, as follows:

(i) *blonde*   = [*alice, phoebe, sarah, liza, amaryllis, belinda, rose, sandra, helen, gertrude, phyllis, daisy*]

(ii) *blueeyed* = [*rose, sandra, helen, gertrude, mavis, vera, elsie, gladys, karen, katrina, claudia, julia*]

(iii) *buxom*   = [*helen, gertrude, phyllis, daisy, anna, daphne, elsie, gladys*]

Figure 12.1 shows a diagram, known as a **Venn diagram**, representing the sets and illustrates the relations between them. The square represents the s *blonde*, the horizontal rectangle the set *blueeyed*, and the vertical rectangle th set *buxom*.

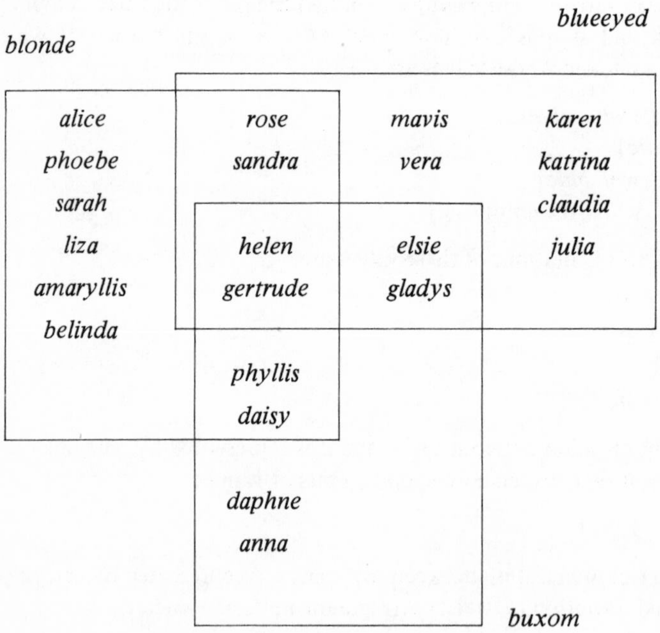

Fig. 12.1 – A Venn diagram illustrating the sets *blonde*, *blueeyed*, and *buxom*.

From the diagram, we can identify at a glance the members of the followir sets.

blonde, blueeyed and *buxom*, that is:

blonde*blueeyed*buxom = [*helen, gertrude*]

blueeyed but neither *blonde* nor *buxom*, that is:

blueeyed − (*blonde* + *buxom*) = [*mavis, vera, karen, katrina, claudia, julia*]

blonde or *buxom*, that is:

blonde + *buxom* = [*alice, phoebe, sarah, liza, amaryllis, belinda, rose, sandra,*
                              helen, gertrude, phyllis, daisy, daphne, anna, elsie, gladys]

12.2.4 Set definitions and declarations of set variables

The syntax of a set definition is:

'type' indentifier '= **set of**' base-type

The base-type may be either a type-identifier, or it may be an actual set, built up as follows:

set   = '[' element-list ']';
element-list = element{ ',' element} | empty;
element   = expression | expression '..' expression;

EXAMPLES

type *primary* = (*red, yellow, blue*);
    colour   = **set of** *primary*;
    digit   = 0..9;
    digitset = **set of** *digit*;
    dayset   = **set of** (*mon, tue, wed, thur, fri, sat, sun*);

var *hue*1, *hue*2, *hue*3 : *colour*;
    *colour*1, *colour*2 : *primary*;
    j, k, s, t : *digit*;
    workday, holiday : *dayset*;

12.2.5 How to use set type variables – case study

Set types can be useful when we are processing entities having a collection of attributes in which we are interested, especially when the attributes are not all mutually exclusive, and especially when we are interested in various different combinations of these attributes. Another factor we need to remember is that there is a machine-dependent size limit upon sets; to fix ideas, we shall assume a size limit of 16. We may summarise the conditions for advantageous use of sets as follows:

(i) There is a collection of entities with at most 16 attributes of interest to be recorded.

(ii) The attributes are not all mutually exclusive.

(iii) We are interested in being able to select entities having particular combinations of these attributes.

Consider a practical example. An estate agent keeps records of a large number of properties in his hands for sale. He finds that in order to select properties of interest to potential buyers, the following property attributes are of interest:

1. Price less than £20,000
2. Price £20,000 to £35,000
3. Price £35,000 t0 £50,000
4. Price above £50,000
5. Freehold
6. Long lease (> 50 years)
7. On a main road
8. A house
9. Semi-detatched
10. Terraced
11. A bungalow
12. A maisonette
13. A flat
14. Entirely ground floor accommodation
15. Central heating
16. A garden
17. 1 main room
18. 2 main rooms
19. 3 main rooms
20. 4 main rooms

A typical requirement from a potential buyer might be for attributes 2, 5, (*not* 7), 13, 14, 18. It is of course possible to do without set types, but the programming would involve many cumbersome boolean expressions and case statements. Can we use set types instead? This example seems fairly well-suited to such treatment, but first there is one obvious difficulty — there are more than 16 attributes.

Is there a way of cutting down the number of attributes without loss of information? In this example there certainly is such a way. First look for a group of attributes which are mutually exclusive. There are two such groups in our example, each having 4 members. They are [1, 2, 3, 4] and [17, 18, 19, 20]. In each of these cases we want to represent 4 different values — it should be clear that this is generally possible using only 2 bits, not 4, since only 2 bits are required to express four different binary values. Only a small amount of ingenuity is required to think of a suitable way of doing this in any particular case.

In the case of [17, 18, 19, 20] we could for example use two attributes only:

(i) Odd number of rooms
(ii) More than two rooms

here are four possible combinations of (i) and (ii), namely both, neither, one,
: the other.

In the case of [1, 2, 3, 4] we could again for example use two attributes
nly:

(a) less than £35,000

(b) Abs (price − £35,000) < £15,000

gain there are four possible combinations giving the four mutually exclusive
tributes we started with. The trick is to replace four mutually exclusive attri-
ites by two overlapping ones. In general, it is always possible to replace 2^m
utually exclusive attributes by m overlapping ones − this is merely a par-
cular application of the fact that 2^m different values may be expressed in
nary, using just m bits.

The type definitions and declarations required for our example are as follows:

type *attributes* = (*under35, near35, freehold, longlease, mainrd, house,*
semi, terraced, bungalow, maisonette, flat, grndlevel,
centralh, garden, oddnumrms, more2rms);

var *include, exclude, interest, choice1* : **set of** *attributes*;

addition, it is assumed that the record type for *property* includes a field called
y *tribs* of type **set of** *attributes*, which is used to record the attributes of the
operty, and that an array *prop* of properties (that is, of type *property*) has
en declared and initialised.

We can initialise *include* and *exclude* to express the typical requirements
eviously described, by the assignments:

include := [*under35, near35, grndlevel, flat*];
exclude := [*mainrd, oddnumrms, more2rms*];

o search for the properties of interest, we can write a loop such as:

```
for k := 1 to max do
  begin
    with prop [k] do
      begin
        if (include < tribs)
        and (exclude*tribs = [ ])
        then
        {write out entire record of property}
      end
  end
```

Notice that the condition for writing a record requires two tests. The first
nsures that the wanted attributes are included, by requiring that *include* is
subset of *tribs*. The second ensures that all the attributes to be excluded

are in fact absent, by requiring that the intersection of *exclude* and *tribs* is t
empty set, [ ]. (Note that it would be insufficient to require merely that *exclu*
is not a subset of *tribs*, by using **not** (*exclude* < *tribs*) because this can be tr
whenever one or some *but not all* of the unwanted attributes are present).

Sometimes, a potential buyer might present alternative requirements, f
example the property must be a flat *or* a maisonette *or* a bungalow. This ki
of requirement can be expressed by assigning the subset of alternatives to a
variable and testing to ensure that its intersection with *tribs* is not empty, f
example:

   *choice*1 := [*flat, maisonette, bungalow*];

and the boolean expression following 'if' in the for loop must be expanded
the addition of:

   and not (*choice*1 * *tribs* = [ ])

(Of course, the initialisation of the set *include* would have to be changed so th
it no longer contained *flat*. The modified program fragment then becomes:

   include := [*under35, near35, grndlevel*];
   exclude := [*mainrd, oddnumrms, more2rms*];

```
   for k := 1 to max do
     begin
       with prop [k] do
         begin
           if (include < tribs)
             and (exclude * tribs = [ ])
             and not (choice1 * tribs = [ ])
           then
             {write out entire record of property}
                    • • •
         end
     end
```

12.3 PROBLEMS

12.3.1

Who are the members of the following sets (using the definitions given
Section 12.2.3):

   (i)   *blueeyed* * *buxom* − *blonde*
   (ii) *blonde* * *blueeyed*
   (iii) *blonde* * *buxom*

What are the values of the following boolean expressions:

(iv) *blueeyed* < (*blueeyed* ∗ *buxom* − *blonde*)

(v) *elsie* **in** (*buxom* + *blonde*)

(vi) (*phyllis* **in** *blueeyed*) = (*phyllis* **in** (*blueeyed* + *buxom*))

12.3.2

Write a complete *expenditure* program as described in Section 8.2, but use an array of records to store the details of each invoice, and use a procedure for each of the main tasks of the program, such as reading in the data for each invoice, for performing the task required by Section 8.4.2, etc.

12.3.3

Write a complete set of programs to serve the needs of the estate agent as described in Section 12.2.5. The programs should include one for updating the file of data (by reading in new properties and deleting properties sold or withdrawn), and another for reading in data asking for particular combinations of attributes and printing appropriate output.

CHAPTER 13

Dynamic data structures – lists

'I've got them on a list –
I've got them on a list –
They'll none of them be missed'

Gilbert and Sullivan

13.1 LISTS

As soon as anyone is in a situation where a significant quantity of data has to be managed, lists are essential. Neither the housewife nor the high-powered executive can manage efficiently without keeping and continually updating lists, or having a secretary to do it. Making a list is part of the essence of organisation, and having made it, probably to re-order it, insert new items – perhaps some items become pointers to sub-lists of their own. A list is a living thing. It grows, it shrinks, twists and assumes new shapes, weaves new links between its items, begets new lists. It is a dynamic structure.

How long is a list? ... as long as the proverbial piece of string. A list is as long as it needs to be. If a new item needs to be added, it may be inserted at the head or somewhere in the middle or it may be tacked on to the end. Unlike all the data structures we have met so far, a list does not have a fixed length, does not have a fixed number of items. It may have as many items as are currently required, including the possibility of no items at all, in which case it is an empty list; but there is no such thing as a full list.

The one indispensible thing about a list is a pointer. A list does not effectively exist unless we know where to find its next item. Every item in a list must be associated with a pointer, a piece of information telling where to find the next item in the list. If there is no next item in the list, because the current item is the last, then the pointer must have the value **nil**. The value **nil** may then be thought of as the address of the non-existent item, and a list *always* consists of *one* or more pointers, each with an associated item. A balanced view is to consider a list as a dynamic ordered collection of zero or more records, each record having a two-part structure, and a pointer which points to the first record, that is, the head of the list:

listheadpointer		record data	pointer to next record
pointer		first record	

The 'record data' might be a Pascal record, or it might be any simple data type such as integer. We are interested in studying the structure of a list, not the substructure of the record data which constitutes each item.

13.2 POINTERS

Because a list structure is dynamic, the individual records of a list cannot be given identifiers, as static variables can be. Instead, each is referenced via the pointer which holds its address.

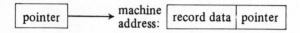

Hence a pointer is itself a special type of variable whose value is a machine address or *reference*. It is always associated with some particular type of record whose address it references. In Pascal, a pointer is said to be *bound* to this type. The type definition required for pointers takes the syntactic form:

    'type' identifier '=' '↑' type-identifier ';'

If, for example, *link* is a pointer type bound to a type *listitem*, then

    type *link* = ↑*listitem*;

(The way to read '↑listitem', mentally or aloud, is 'pointer to listitem'). Of course we should need to define *listitem* too. If its record data is simply integer, then:

    type *listitem* = **record**
                value : *integer*;
                listptr : *link*
        end

Having made our type definitions, we need some variables. Firstly, as previously stated, no list can exist without a listhead pointer. It is also useful to be able to 'keep the place' in the list one is processing, so we declare:

    var *listhead, currentitem, lastitem* : *link*;

and one of the first things we should do in our program is to initialise these by the assignments:

        listhead := **nil**;
    currentitem := **nil**;
      lastitem := **nil**;

We now have an empty list, and two placemarkers to make sure we cannot lose our place in it!

3 OPERATIONS ON POINTER VALUES

at operations can be carried out upon pointer type values in Pascal? These
ues are machine addresses. We need to be able to *use* these, but need not
ow their actual values, and in fact there are basically three kinds of operations
ich can be performed with pointer variables:

(i) comparison
(ii) assignment
(iii) evaluation.

often want to know whether two pointer variables have the same value, that
whether they are pointing to the same location, and we can do this using the
ational operators '=' (equals), and '<>' (notequals). For example, if x and y
pointer variables of the same type then $(x = y)$, $(x <> y)$ are both valid
olean expressions which have the value *true* or *false*.

When we assign the value of one pointer to another, for example:

$x := y$

value being assigned is the store location of a record. A store location is
netimes called an address, a machine address, or a reference. It is very like a
ne. It refers to another variable. If x is a pointer variable whose value is a
erence to some other variable, we shall sometimes want to use this value,
t is, to use the variable being referenced.

In fact the only way we *can* refer to, or *use* a variable is by denoting the
ue of the pointer variable which refers to it. In other words we must *evaluate*
pointer variable, because its value is the reference we wish to use. The
erator which does this is the '↑', and to evaluate a pointer variable, the '↑'
placed immediately following the identifier of the pointer variable. For
mple, if x is a pointer variable then the referenced variable it points at is
oted by $x↑$, and if $x↑$ is a record, and one of its fields is a, then that field
enoted by:

$x↑.a$

ile another field, called b, is denoted by:

$x↑.b$

if a, b are of type *integer*, we can assign integer values such as 53, 199 in the
inary way:

$x↑.a := 53;$
$x↑.b := 199$

e record $x↑$ may also have a pointer field c, to which we can assign values of
same type, for example:

$x↑.c := y$

However, note that

$x\uparrow.c := y\uparrow$

does *not* make sense, though

$x\uparrow.c := y\uparrow.c$

does make sense. (The way to read '$x\uparrow$', mentally or aloud, is 'x reference').

13.4 GROWING A DYNAMIC STRUCTURE

As we have seen, dynamic variables do not have identifiers, only pointers, that references to them, and this is why they are called referenced variables. It therefore clear that there cannot be any question of declaring them in t ordinary way. Rather, having previously defined the type, we should expect be able to generate a variable at any required point in the program; and this exactly what we can do. Pascal provides a standard procedure *new* which tak a pointer variable as its parameter. When it is called, for example:

   new(*listhead*)

a new variable of type *listitem* is provided, and the address of this variable automatically assigned to *listhead*. The system 'knows' that the type of variat required is *listitem*, because that is the type to which *link*, the type of listhea is bound. Keeping lists up to date is very important, so we should update o markers pointing to the current and last items in our list. At the moment the two items are identical so we require:

   currentitem := *listhead*;
   listitem := *listhead*;

Although we now have a list with one variable to represent the one item in : we have not yet assigned any values to this variable, that is to the record type *listitem* which we have generated. This record is referenced not by a identifier but by the reference or pointer variable which serves instead of name. We can assign values to the two fields by:

   listhead$\uparrow$.*value*   := 97531; {97531 is arbitrary}
   listhead$\uparrow$.*listptr* := **nil**;

It is important to avoid confusion between *listhead* and *listhead*$\uparrow$. The differen is that between the name of a reference and a reference. We have a static variab called *listhead* whose value, that is, contents, is a reference to another variabl called *listhead*$\uparrow$, (pronounced *listheadreference*).

   Diagramatically:

| listhead : | listhead$\uparrow$ | ⟶ | listhead$\uparrow$: | 97531 | nil |

ach box represents a store location, with its name or reference proceeding it, erminated by a colon. The contents of each box is its value.

In other words, *listhead* is the name of a pointer variable while *listhead*↑ is he name of a record which *listhead* points at. For any reader who is unsure bout this, a pointer to further explanation is (Section 1.2).

The **with** statement may be used with referenced variables just as with other ecords. Hence the two assignments to our listitem could have been written.

```
.  with listhead↑ do
      begin
         value  := 97531;
         listptr := nil
      end {with statement}
```

)f course, the value 97531 assigned to *value* is quite arbitrary − we might nstead have used:

```
read (value)
```

o read in any integer value of data.

3.4.1 Making a list

suppose we now tackle the task of reading in some data and constructing a ist. We should like a procedure *readlist* and a procedure *writelist*. We already now something about the structure of our data, so we shall start by jotting lown suitable program declarations.

```
type link = ↑listitem;
     listitem = record
                     value : integer;
                     pointer : link
                 end;
  var listhead, item : link;
```

The central task is that of adding a new record to an existing list. Each ime we do this, we must:

(i) obtain a new storage location, using *new*;
(ii) read in the next piece of data.

each time we use *new*, we have to supply an actual parameter of type *link*, and •efore we can use it again, we must update the address of the *link* parameter. To start with we have no dynamic storage. We do have our two *link* type variables isthead and *item*. We shall use *item* to keep our place as we move through the ist, so the first two instructions required would appear to be:

```
new (listhead);
item := listhead;
```

Our store situation can now be shown diagrammatically using DA to stand fo
Dynamic Storage Address.

Now we can read in the first data item, value1

> *read*(*item*↑.*value*)

and the effect on our store is shown by:

DA1 : | value1 | |

Of course, the only way we can refer in the program to the record whose value i
value1 is by using its reference, which is the contents of our *link* variable *item*
that is, *item*↑. When we obtain our next dynamic storage location we want th
new address written into the pointer field of the record we refer to as *item*↑
and this is achieved by the instruction:

> *new*(*item*↑.*pointer*)

Our storage situation is now:

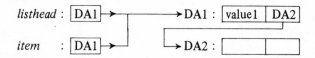

And now we update the address stored in *item* so that it points to DA2, by th
instruction:

> *item* := *item*↑.*pointer*

The storage situation is now:

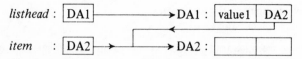

and the reference for DA2 is *item*↑, so that we are now able to read in ou
second data item by the instruction:

> *read*(*item*↑.*value*)

Collecting up our instructions to date and putting them together, we have:

new(listhead);
item := listhead,
read(item↑.value);

new(item↑.pointer);
item := item↑.pointer;
read(item↑.value;

The first three instructions are only slightly different from the second three, and this is because we start with the *link* variable *listhead* which is left pointing permanently to the beginning of the list. The second group of three instructions will need to be repeated every time we add another data value to the list, until, in the course of reading, we reach the end of file. In other words we want to construct a loop out of this second group of instructions, and we can do so as follows:

```
while not eof do
    begin
        new(item↑.pointer);
        item := item↑.pointer;
        read(item↑.value)
    end;
```

he last record added to the list has nothing at all written in its pointer field, and to indicate that it is the last record of the list, we should assign **nil** to this *nk*:

item↑.pointer := nil

To print out the list of values, we must of course start with the record pointed at by *listhead*. Obviously we shall want a loop, so we can start by copying the reference contained in *listhead* into *item*. Our loop should continue so long the current reference is not **nil**, for example:

```
while item <> nil do
    begin
        write(item↑.value);
        item := item↑.pointer
    end;
```

are now ready to write the complete program which reads and writes a list.

```
program listexample(input, output);
type link = ↑listitem;
    listitem = record value : integer;
                        pointer : link
               end;
var listhead : link;
```

```
procedure listread (var head : link);
var next : link; buffer : integer;
  begin
    new (head);
    next := head;
    read (next↑.value);
      if not eof then read (buffer);
      while not eof do
        begin
          new (next↑.pointer);
          next := next↑.pointer;
          next↑.value := buffer;
          read (buffer)
        end;
      next↑.pointer := nil
  end {of listread};

procedure listwrite (head : link);
var next : link;
  begin
    next := head;
      while not (next = nil) do
        begin
          writeln (next↑.value)
          next := next↑.pointer
        end
  end {listwrite}; {end of declarations}
begin {start of program block}
    listhead := nil;
    listread (listhead);
    listwrite (listhead)
end.
```

13.4.2 Deleting an item

Assuming that we have a linked list whose first record is pointed at by a pointer variable called *listhead*, we may wish to remove from the list the record whose value field contains a certain value.

We shall have to step through the list searching for the record to be removed. As we search, we must ensure that we save the pointer reference to the predecessor of each record until after we have compared its value field with the value we are looking for. Using an integer type variable *wanted* for this purpose and two place pointers *current* and *next*, the condition we want satisfied is:

$next↑.value = wanted$

ere

next = *current↑. pointer*

then have a situation as shown in Fig. 13.1. All we have to do in order to move the record whose value field equals *wanted*, is to change the value of *rent↑.pointer* so that it points to *next↑. pointer,* that is:

current↑. pointer := *next↑. pointer*

designing the sequence of instructions to carry out the search, we must ensure t we evaluate a pointer and check that this value is not **nil** before attempting use it as a reference. And before we can write a loop, we must copy the value *listhead* into *current*. Each time we compare *wanted* with the next value, we her delete it, or move the pointers along one place through the list ready for next time round the loop.

Before reading the function provided, the reader is strongly urged to try to te it for himself:

```
function deleteitem (var listhead : link; wanted :integer) : boolean;
var next, current : link;
    deleted : boolean;
  begin
    deleted := false;
      if (listhead <> nil)
      then
        begin
          next := listhead↑. pointer;
          if (listhead↑. value = wanted)
          then
            begin
              listhead := next {drop unwanted first item};
              deleted := true
            end
          else
            begin
              current := listhead;
                while (next <> nil) and (not deleted) do
                  begin
                    if (next↑. value = wanted)
                    then
                      begin
                        current↑. pointer := next↑. pointer;
                        deleted := true
                      end
```

```
                else current := next {move current along};
                next := next↑. pointer {move next along}
            end
        end
    end;
        deleteitem := deleted
    end {of function deleteitem};
```

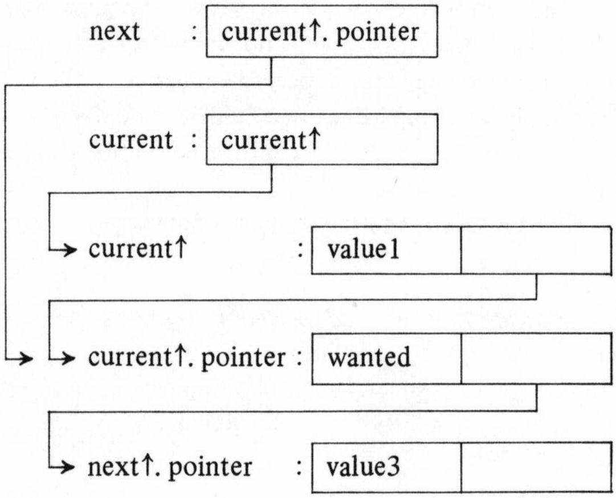

next   : current↑. pointer

current : current↑

↳ current↑   : value1

↳ ↳ current↑. pointer : wanted

↳ next↑. pointer   : value3

Fig. 13.1.

13.4.3 Inserting an item

Inserting an item into a list at a particular place is clearly a very similar exerc
to deleting an item. However, there are several possible variations: the inserti
may be required immediately before or immediately after a specified item, oi
may be required (and specified) between two given items. In any case, no mat
how its insertion has been specified, we have to find the *two* items already
the list, between which the insertion is to be placed, because, once we have fou
them, there are two operations to be carried out, one concerning the precedi
item and the other concerning the following item.

The preceding item must have its pointer field changed so that it no lon
points to the following item, but to the inserted item. But before losing t
reference to the following item, that pointer value must be copied to the poin
field of the inserted item.

13.4.4 Moving an item in a list or swapping two items

No new considerations enter into these operations, because they can be built
from deletion and insertion. Deletion and insertion are the building blocks f
the apparently more complex operations on lists. However, they are not actua
more complex, merely longer.

13.4.5 Making a list into a ring

Sometimes we want a list constructed in the form of a continuous ring or circle, so that the 'last' item in the list points to the 'first'. It is a simple matter to arrange this. We still need to keep a listhead pointer, so that we have a reference which enables us to enter the ring, but the pointer field of what would normally be the last item, instead of being assigned the **nil** value is assigned the value of the listhead pointer, thus completing the ring (see Fig. 13.2).

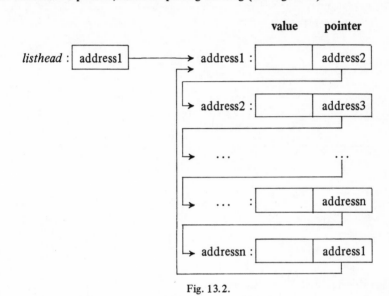

Fig. 13.2.

13.4.6 Nodes and trees

A tree is merely a list with branches. Sometimes one has data whose natural structure is heirarchical. An example from everyday life is a family tree. Tree structure occurs quite commonly in many forms; a particularly simple form of tree is the binary tree. In a binary tree, each node points to precisely two other nodes. Sometimes the terminal nodes, which do not point to any more nodes, are called leaves. The node from which the tree structure emanates is naturally called the root. The tree is called 'binary' because each node has two branches. A tree structure can be used very effectively to express an ordering of data.

Figure 13.3 shows a binary tree which exhibits such as use. It has the property that the value of each node is greater than the value of any node to its left and less than the value of any node to its right. The entire tree contains 15 nodes, but searching for the presence of some particular value requires at worst 4 comparisons. For example, to find say 37, we carry out a procedure as follows:

(i) if 37 = 43
   then we have found what we are looking for
   otherwise
      if 37 < 43
      then move to left node
      otherwise move to right node.
(ii) repeat (i), substituting the value of the new node for 43
(iii) repeat (ii)
(iv) repeat (iii)

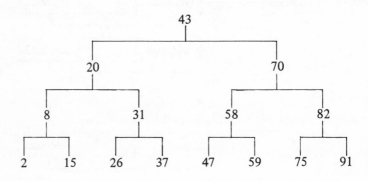

Fig. 13.3.

The algorithm in Pascal is as follows:

```
program tree(output);
type link = ↑node;
      node = record
                   value : integer;
                   leftpointer : link;
                   rightpointer : link
              end;

var rootpointer, next : link;
{we shall assume that the tree has already been constructed and has the data
data as illustrated}
```

{A boolean function *present*, which checks the presence or otherwise of a given integer value in the tree, can be written as follows:}

```
function present(val : integer; pointer : link) : boolean;
var item : integer; found : boolean;
   begin
```

```
        found := false;
            while (pointer <> nil) and not found do
                begin
                  item := pointer↑.value;
                    if val = item
                    then found := true
                    else
                        if val < item
                        then pointer := pointer↑.leftpointer
                        else pointer := pointer↑.rightpointer
                end;
            present := found
    end {of function present};
    begin
        {remainder of program}
    end.
```

The basic idea underlying this search algorithm (taken together with the
way the data is structured) is identical with the idea behind the binary search
program in Section 7.4.2 called *binsearch*. The difference lies in the way the
sorted data is arranged.

3.4.7 Dead wood and garbage collection

In any program using large dynamic data structures, new lists may be growing
and shrinking on a large scale. If store which is no longer wanted is not re-used,
the total store required may grow beyond reasonable bounds. In order to avoid
this, we can return unwanted dynamic storage by using the standard procedure:

$$dispose(p)$$

which is the inverse of *new*(*p*). The actual parameter *p* must be a pointer type
variable in both cases. The effect of *dispose*(*p*) is to return the location *p*↑ to
the system – it is then no longer available within the program.

An alternative to using *dispose* is to collect unwanted locations in a separate
list of 'free', unused store and to transfer items back into lists in use when
required. The re-use or return of unwanted dynamic store is commonly known
as garbage collection.

3.5 PROBLEMS
3.5.1

Extend and amend the program *listexample* given in Section 13.4.1 to include
procedures for deletion, insertion, and swapping of items, and for searching to
see if an item is present. Write a program body and supply data to test and
demonstrate that all procedures appear to work correctly.

13.5.2

Using the same program, write a procedure to sort the list into ascending order of its value fields. Amend the program to demonstrate the action.

13.5.3

Write a program *growtree*, which reads in a sequence of unsorted integer values and stores them in the binary tree structure described in Section 13.4.6, so that the function *present* can be used to find them. (Hint: make the first item the root of the tree, and then use a slightly amended version of *present* to find where to put each new item).

CHAPTER 14

Dynamic program structures – recursion

A mathematician called 'Ben',
Often wanted some function of *n*.
If it couldn't be done,
He'd try *n* minus one,
And he'd do it ag'en and ag'en!

See recursion

14.1 RECURSIVE DEFINITIONS

A recursive definition is fun, just like the merry-go-round at a funfair. It allows us to indulge in that 'awful sin' we were taught to avoid by our English teachers at school, the definition that goes round in a circle and comes back to itself. The titilating bit is that it works!

According to classical tradition, all logical systems start with a set of axioms, sometimes called 'self-evident truths', and are built up from definitions which are based, always, upon combinations of previous definitions and the axioms. One of the disadvantages of this approach is that sometimes self-evident truths turn out to be erroneous, whilst some apparently wildly hilarious idea, like relativity, which is certainly not self-evident, seems to work. Furthermore, mathematicians have discovered time and again that the detailed investigation of logical systems based upon very peculiar 'axioms' sometimes turns out to be a very interesting exercise.

The truth about definitions is that they are *always* circular, because, wherever you start, you start with words, and it is difficult to define those words except in terms of words. There is an old proverb — 'If you can't beat them, join them', which we might perhaps paraphrase as 'If you can't avoid a circular definition, relax and enjoy it!'.

However, like any good game, the recursion game has rules. (We certainly don't allow *any* old circular definition into *this* club.) To be a recursive definition, you have to qualify. Every recursive definition is a definition of a class of entities, and has two parts, which usually take the following form:

(i) *Fred* is a member of the class we are defining.
(ii) If *Jimmy* is a member, so is *Jimmy's* ------.

The string of six dashes, '------', is not a polite way of printing a swearword, it stands for something which has some definite relationship with *Jimmy*. This relationship is the essence of the definition. For example, we could substitute '*father*' for '------'. The class defined would then be the entire line of male ancestors of Fred (and of course Fred himself).

Another example:

  (i) The integer value, 1 is a member of the class we are defining.
  (ii) If the integer value k is a member, then so is the value $2*k$.

This is a definition of the class of non-negative integer powers of 2.

So far this probably seems too simple, and nothing is ever worth learning unless it is just a little bit difficult at least. Suppose we rewrite the last two definitions using BNF. We might get something like these definitions:

  (1) Fred-or-forebear = *'Fred'*
                 | **'father of'** *Fred*
                 | **'father of'** Fred-or-forebear;
  (2) a-power-of-two = '1' | '2*' a-power-of-two;

Of course, our examples so far are rather trivial. Let us look at a recursive definition of something more worthwhile. In Chapter 5 we introduced the **while** loop (Section 5.1.2) and explained its meaning by examples, by a flow chart, and a trance table. The **while** loop statement always has the form:

  while BE **do** ST

where BE stands for boolean expression, and ST stands for statement. We can *define* a statement of the above form recursively by saying it is exactly equivalent to the following:

  if BE
  then
    begin
      ST;
      while BE **do** ST
    end

First of all let us work through this and see what happens – you will see that if BE is *false* then nothing happens at all. That is correct. It is just what happens with a **while** statement. On the other hand, if BE is **true** the first time it is evaluated than ST is executed at least once – again correct, just as in a **while** statement. Immediately following that execution of ST we meet the very **while** statement we are supposed to be defining! Is that useless? Well our definition at least tells us how to start – we plug in the entire definition again – that is, we expand the **while** statement into a sequence which starts:

  if BE
  then ...

Here we go round the merry-go-round, but who cares! If BE is *false* we unfortunately have to stop, but if it is **true**, then round we go again, executing ST for the second time, and then when we meet the **while** statement once more, why all we need to do is to expand it into a sequence which starts:

if BE
then ...

just as we did before. The expansion of the **while** statement happens automatically every time we evaluate BE and find it to be *true*, and stops just as soon as we find it to be *false*.

Is this a recursive definition — is it a member of the club? Does it have the form we said all recursive definitions should have? Yes it does, but we have varied the notation slightly. We can easily rewrite it in the Fred and Jimmy form, or even in BNF — here goes:

Fred and Jimmy form:

   (i) '**if** BE **then** ST1' is a possible form
  (ii) If ST2 is a possible form, then so is:

        '**if** BE **then**
            begin
               ST1;
               ST2
          end'

In BNF:

    while-statement = '**if**' BE
                  '**then**' ST
                  | '**if**' BE
                  '**then**'
                  '**begin**' ST ';'
                  while-statement '**end**';

But this is a definition not of a syntax rule but of the *meaning* of a while statement.

14.2 RECURSIVE SUB-PROGRAMS

What is a recursive sub-program? It is a sub-program which directly corresponds to and implements a recursive definition. We shall start with a very simple example, so trivial that there is nothing in it apart from its recursiveness. It is a procedure to write blank lines. First we write a non-recursive version, *nonreclines*, and then a recursive version, *reclines*, as follows:

```
procedure nonreclines(k : integer);
var j : integer;
   begin
      for j := 1 to k do writeln
   end;

procedure reclines(k : integer);
   begin
      if k > 1 then reclines(k − 1);
      writeln
   end
```

Unlike the non-recursive version, the recursive version has *no* loop. Instead, its body contains a call of itself. This call in the conditional statement is activated only if $k > 1$. The call generates a new block of program, with its own new scope, its own new working space, its own virtual existence. The formal parameter k is called by value, and therefore represents a local variable *with its scope local to the procedure in which it is invoked.* Each time the procedure is called a *new* invocation takes place, a *new* block is entered which constitutes the scope of a *new* local variable corresponding to the formal parameter k. This process takes place at run-time. At compilation time neither the machine nor a human intelligence can tell how many times the procedure may be invoked at run-time. Thus the creation of new program blocks at run-time is a dynamic process. The recursive creation of new program blocks is a dynamic programming structure.

If we try to make a trace table to show the effect of recursive procedure, we shall be obliged to rule and provide headings for a new set of columns corresponding to all its local variables (both declared, and formal parameters called by value) each time the procedure is invoked. In the case of *reclines*, there is only one local variable, the formal parameter k. It would be difficult to follow a trace table of *reclines*, simply because we cannot *see* its output, which consists entirely of blank lines. We shall therefore vary it slightly so that it produces some output that illuminates its activity. A good cheap supply of illumination comes from the stars, so we shall arrange for the output of '1 *' on the first line, '2 *' on the second line, and so on, and so we have:

```
procedure starline(k : integer);
   begin
      if k > 1 then starline(k − 1);
      writeln(k, '*')
   end;
```

That is the static representation of the sub-program. But if a call of this procedure is made, using an actual parameter value, say, of 3, that is:

starline(3)

hen a dynamic equivalent program can be written. In order to distinguish more easily between the different scopes of the different local variables all called k, each is given a separate column in the following representation of a dynamic expansion of the call, *starline*(3), incorporated into a trace table (see Table 14.1).

Table 14.1 – Trace Table for procedure call, *starline*(3).

Instruction	Effect — block 1		block 2		block 3		Output
	$k>1$	k	$k>1$	k	$k>1$	k	
starline(3) {enter block 1}; **if** $k>1$	*true*	3					
then {block 2 now entered}							
starline$(k-1)$; **if** $k>1$			*true*	2			
then {block 3 now entered}							
starline$(k-1)$; **if** $k>1$ **then** {not executed}; *writeln*$(k,\,'*')$ {exit from block 3 continue in block 2};					*false*	1	1 *
writeln$(k,\,'*')$ {exit from block 2 continue in block 1};							2 *
writeln$(k,\,'*')$ {exit from block 1 return to main program}							3 *

14.3 EXAMPLES OF USE OF RECURSION

14.3.1 Pascal's triangle

The programming language Pascal is named after the great French mathematician, Blaise Pascal, who was born in 1623, and died in 1662. His name is now firmly attached to a well-known triangle of integers, whose values are of interest in part of the study of probability. The triangle has a certain fascination of its own and the first six rows and columns are reproduced in Table 14.2. Let us call this array C, and identify each component value by a pair of subscripts, first row then column. Then we can see that for example $C_{5,3} = 10$, that is the value in the 5th row and 3rd column is 10. The facinating property of the table arises from the relations between is component values. In particular, it can be seen that each value is the sum of the value immediately above it and the value immediately to the left of that.

Table 14.2 – Pascal's triangle.

	0	1	2	3	4	5
0	1					
1	1	1				
2	1	2	1			
3	1	3	3	1		
4	1	4	6	4	1	
5	1	5	10	10	5	1

Note that the function is defined only when (row $\geqslant$ column $\geqslant 0$).

For example:

$$C_{5,3} = C_{4,3} + C_{4,2}$$

Or more generally,

$$C_{j,k} = C_{j-1,k} + C_{j-1,k-1}$$

given that:

$C_{j,0} = 1$ for all the values of j

and

$C_{j,j} = 1$ for all the values of j

This is obviously a perfectly good recursive definition of the function $C(j,k)$, and it is a fairly simple matter to write such a Pascalian function as follows:

```
function C(row, column : integer) : integer;
   begin
      if (column = 0)
```

```
      or (row = column)
   then C := 1
else
   C := C(row − 1, column) + C(row − 1, column − 1)
end;
```

14.3.2 Reversal

A recursive definition often seems to define a thing in terms of something which preceded it. So it should be particularly useful in circumstances where we already know all the values preceding the one of current interest. It may so happen that we have some data which has been sorted, and written onto a sequential file, but we particularly want this order exactly reversed, for example we want a data sequence of integer values in ascending instead of descending order. A recursive procedure will do this very simply indeed, and because of its dynamic properties, it will work for a sequence of unknown length.

```
procedure reverseorder;
var val : integer;
   begin
      if not eof
      then
         begin
            read(val);
            reverseorder;
            write(val)
         end
```

14.3.3 The Towers of Hanoi

An attractive myth tells how, in a sacred temple, there are three needles of diamonds, on one of which originally rested 64 golden discs, all of different sizes, forming a pyramidical tower, the needle passing through a central hole in each disc. The monks of the temple have the task of moving all the discs to one of the other two needles, but they must observe the sacred laws, which do not permit a larger disc ever to rest upon a smaller one, and which allow only one disc at a time to be moved. When the task is completed, and all 64 discs have been moved, says the myth, the world will come to an end.

Mythology apart, the problem is not without interest, and you will find it instructive to try it for yourself. As you may not have three diamond needles and sixty-four golden discs handy, they can be dispensed with, and discs of baser metal used instead. Also, you may not have enough spare time to occupy yourself with this problem until the end of the world, and therefore it is perhaps advisable to reduce the number of discs to four or five. Coins of ½p, 1p, 5p, 2p and 10p will be found to have conveniently graded sizes. Thus for an outlay of

18½p only, you too can play at the Towers of Hanoi. It must be admitted that the satisfaction and enjoyment derived using the substitute equipment does not match the thrill of using the pukkah diamond needles and golden discs in the temple at Hanoi, but if you are too disappointed you can always drown your sorrows by appropriate use of the 18½p.

The sequence of moves required is tricky. A useful technique is to try first with 2 discs, then with 3, next with 4, and at last with 5. By this time you should begin to recognise the pattern in the sequence of moves and perhaps to see that the pattern is recursive (see Table 14.3). The minimum number of individual moves required to transfer n discs is 2 to the nth power, minus 1. $(2^{63} - 1)$ is greater than 10^{19}. You can try 64 discs if you like, but if you make one move per second, and don't make any mistakes, it will take you more than a hundred thousand million years to complete the transfer. Even if you make a million moves per second, it would still take a hundred thousand years, so be careful how many discs you tackle even in a simulated solution on a computer.

Table 14.3.

Number of discs	Number of moves
1	1
2	3
3	7
4	15
5	31
•	•
•	•
•	•
64	$2^{63} - 1$

Solving the problem in principle is very easy using the recursive method. The argument follows the expected pattern and is as follows:

(i) To transfer a pile containing just 1 disc is trivially simple.
(ii) To transfer a pile containing n discs, first move $(n - 1)$ discs, to the third position (not the final destination).
    Move the remaining 1 disc to the final destination. Lastly, move the $(n - 1)$ discs to the final destination.

The only problem is how to move $(n - 1)$ discs. But we tackle this in exactly the same way as we did for n discs — but this time we are left with the problem for $(n - 2)$ discs. We are now riding the recursive merry-go-round, ad each time round it, the problem is reduced to the transfer of 1 less disc — $(n-3), (n-4), \ldots 3, 2, 1$ — bingo! We know how to transfer 1. Therefore we now know how to transfer 2, therefore we know how to transfer 3, $\ldots (n-4),$ $(n-3), (n-2), (n-1), n$ — problem solved.

The basic piece of program required must have the form:

procedure *transfer*$(n : integer)$;
  if $n = 1$
  then movedisc from position 1 to position 2
  else
    begin
      transfer$(n-1)$ from position 1 to position 3;
      movedisc from position 1 to position 2;
      transfer$(n-1)$ from position 3 to position 1
    end

Of course this is not yet a Pascal procedure, but it is beginning to look like one. It is a serviceable first specification of what we need, and highlights immediately a small problem of how we should refer to the different positions. If we identify them by integer values 1, 2, and 3, and introduce integer variables *start*, *finish* and *other*, this may be convenient. Is it? Can we express *other* easily in terms of *start* and *finish*? Yes we can, because if each refers to a different position, then it is always true that:

$$start + finish + other = 6$$

Clearly, the procedure *transfer* should have three parameters: *start*, *finish*, and *n*, where *n* is the number of discs to transfer. We don't really need a separate procedure for moving 1 disc — it is simply what *transfer* does when $n = 1$, but it is worth 'pretending' for the moment that there is an instruction '*move*1' which we can expand later, so that we can make a shot at a real Pascal procedure for transferring *n* discs.

procedure *transfer*$(n, start, finish : integer)$;
var *other* : *integer*;
  begin
    if $n = 1$
    then *move*1
    else
      begin
        other $:= 6 - start - finish$;
        transfer$(n-1, start, other)$;
        *move*1;
        transfer$(n-1, other, finish)$;
      end
  end

The most simple thing to substitute for *move*1 is a *writeln* instruction givin
the required move to be made, for example:

    writeln('move disc from position', *start*, 'to', *finish*)

The complete program, with some minor tidying up, becomes:

```
program hanoi(input, output);
type position = 1..3;
var k : integer;
  procedure transfer(discs : integer; start, finish : position);
  var other : position;
    begin
      if discs = 1
      then writeln(' move disc from position', start, 'to', finish)
      else
        begin
          other := 6 − start − finish;
          transfer(discs − 1, start, other);
          writeln('move disc from position', start, 'to', finish);
          transfer (discs − 1, other, finish)
        end
    end {of transfer};
    begin {main program}
      read(k, start, finish);
      writeln(' Towers of Hanoi Program');
      writeln;
      writeln(' Instructions for transfer of', k, 'discs');
      writeln;
      transfer(k, start, finish)
    end.
```

14.3.4 Recursive definition of arithmetic operators for positive integers

The following examples are given because their simplicity helps to demonstrat
the essentials of recursion. Of course, one would not dream of using them fo
actual computation, though they are of interest as rigorous definitions of th
operations of addition, multiplication, and exponentiation for positive integer:
using only the *pred* and *suc* functions.

In order to keep the function declarations simple, it is assumed that a $<$
(It is not difficult to modify the functions so that they work without th
assumption being true).

```
function add(a, b : integer) : integer;
  begin
    if a = 0
    then add := b
    else add := add(pred(a), succ(b))
  end;

function mult(x, y : integer) : integer;
  begin {definition of x*y}
    if x = 0
    then mult := 0
    else mult := add(y, mult(pred(x), y))
    {that is, mult := y + mult(pred(x), y)}
  end;

function exp(u, v : integer) : integer;
  begin
  {definition of u↑v}
    if v = 0
    then exp := 1
    else exp := mult(u, exp(u, pred(v)))
  end;
```

14.4 PROBLEMS

14.4.1

The Shorter Oxford English Dictionary defines a 'descendant' as 'one who is descended from an ancestor', and 'descend' (in this context) as 'to spring from an ancestor'. It defines ancestor as 'one from whom a person is descended, either the father or mother'. Can you devise a better definition, in English, of 'descendant'?

14.4.2

Try putting the definition you produced in answer to Problem 14.4.1 into BNF.

14.4.3

The function C given in Section 14.3.1 is not a very efficient algorithm, because it evaluates the same quantities many times. In the evaluation of the call $C(6,3)$, how many times is $C(2,3)$ evaluated?

14.4.4

Using the formula for the minimum number of moves necessary to solve the Towers of Hanoi problem given in Section 14.3.3, estimate the maximum

number of disks that can sensibly be read in as data to the **program** *han*
assuming the computer takes say 10 milliseconds to make one move, and t
program is to run to completion within say 20 seconds.

14.4.5

Write a recursive Pascal **function** *subtract*(*a, b* : *integer*) : *integer*, whose res
is b — a. Assume that b >= a >= 0. You are not allowed to use any of t
arithmetic operators.

14.4.6

Write a non-recursive Pascal functions for *add*, *mult*, and *exp* which do not u
the arithmetic operators '+', '—', '*', but use the standard functions *pred* a
succ.

14.4.7

Write a recursive Pascal procedure *recbinsearch*, which uses the method
binsearch (see Section 7.4.2) to search an ordered integer array, and produc
the same results as *binsearch*.

CHAPTER 15

Advanced use of parameters

'That's a great deal to make one word mean', Alice said in a thoughtful tone. 'When I make a word do a lot of work like that', said Humpty Dumpty, 'I always pay it extra.'

Lewis Carroll

Function and procedure parameters can be made to work overtime in Pascal. The extra cost is thought and care, but these may be amply repaid.

15.1 CALL BY NAME AND CALL BY VALUE

In Section 10.2.2 a brief introduction was given to call by name. Here we shall look in more detail at the essential differences between name and value parameters, and at the factors which determine our choice of which to use.

15.1.1 Actual and formal parameters

When a sub-program (procedure or function) is declared, the identifiers used to denote its parameters are said to be *formal* parameters. When the sub-program is called, the parameters actually passed to it are said to be its *actual* parameters. For example, in Section 9.2, the function heading:

function *squareroot* (*a, max* : *real*) : *real*;

has two formal parameters, *a* and *max*, both of type *real*. If we write function calls in our program, such as:

squareroot (*x*, 0.0001);

or

squareroot (931.6 + *sin* (*y*), *epsilon*);

or

squareroot (37, 100 * *epsilon*);

then each of the six expressions:

x, 0.0001, 931.6 + *sin* (*y*),
epsilon, 37, 100 * *epsilon*

is an *actual* parameter.

Once a sub-program has been declared, its *formal* parameters are fixed, but different *actual* parameters may be used each time it is called into use. When we say that the formal parameters are fixed, we are talking about names, not values. Every formal parameter is a name, whether it is a name parameter or a value parameter.

It is the actual parameter which is a value in the case of call by value, and a name in the case of call by name.

This is because the parameter-passing mechanism called into play on entry to a sub-program is quite different for the two cases of call by *name* and *value*. In call by value, the formal parameter is the name of a local variable to which the value of the expression used as actual parameter is automatically assigned. Using a formal value parameter is tantamount to the *declaration* of a *local variable* of the type specified.

On the other hand, in the case of call by name, the formal parameter is merely a local name for whatever *global* variable is used as actual parameter whenever the sub-program is called into use. Hence, passing an *expression* as an actual parameter in call by name makes no sense. What is required is a *variable* name. On entry to the sub-program, there is no automatic declaration of a local variable — the required variable already exists, globally. The formal parameter is merely a local, dummy name which is used within the sub-program as a substitute for the name of the actual parameter. Assignment to such a parameter within the sub-program is actually assignment to the global variable used as a corresponding actual parameter. For example, consider the following program:

```
program nameandvalue (input, output);
var x, y : real;
procedure egname (var u : real);
  begin
    u := 100 * u
  end;
procedure egvalue (v : real);
  begin
    v := 100 * v
  end;
begin {main program}
  x := 1.5;
  y := 2.5;
  write (x);
  egname (x).
  writeln (x);
  write (y);
  egvalue (y);
  writeln (y)
end.
```

The output from this program will be:

```
1.5     150
2.5     2.5
```

ɔu will see that, although *egname* and *egvalue* contain identical statements,
eir effect is different — calling *egname* changes the value of *x*, but calling
alue leaves the value of *y* undisturbed.

In the two procedure calls, *egname*(*x*) and *egvalue*(*y*), the actual parameters
ay appear to be a variable in each case, but this is not so. In the first call,
is a variable name, and what is actually passed is the store address of the
riable called *x*. In the second call, *y* is an expression, and what is passed is
e value possessed by the variable *y*; this is found when the expression is
aluated.

If the intention behind using a parameter is the communication of a value
ɔm inside the sub-program out to the external enclosing program block, then
e formal parameter must be a name parameter, specified in the parameter list
the same way as **var** *u*, in *egname*. A formal parameter must be preceded by
r if call by name is intended.

An example of the use of call by name is given by the following procedure.

procedure *swap*(**var** *a, b* : *integer*);
var *temp* : *integer*;
   begin
      temp := *a*;
      a := *b*;
      b := *temp*
   end {of swap};

ιe procedure call *swap*(*x*, *y*), where *x*, *y* are integer variables, will have the
fect of swapping their values. Its effect would be zero if **var** were omitted
ɔm the procedure heading.

5.1.2 An array as parameter

ɔrmal parameters may be arrays, and these may be *name* or *value* parameters.
ιe same parameter passing mechanisms apply as to other variable types, but in
⋅me respects the effects are amplified. If an array has, say, 1000 components,
ιd an actual array of correct type is used as actual parameter, the effect on
ιtry to the sub-program is that a local array is declared, and the 1000 com-
ɔnent values are copied across from the actual parameter to the local array
ɔrresponding to the formal parameter. This copying is automatic and hidden,
ιd so is the requirement for 1000 additional store locations. These costs are
ιl and should be recognised. This is not to say that an array should never be
lled by value, merely that it should not be called by value *needlessly*. Call by
ⅎlue may be necessary to protect the values of the original array, which might
⋅ changed by the sub-program if call by name were used instead of call by
ⅎlue.

When an array parameter is used, it should be remembered that the typ specification fixes the dimensions of the array. Arrays of different dimensio are not the same type in Pascal. For example, a procedure heading may b declared as:

procedure *arrayproc* (*g* : *h*);

where the program contains a type declaration:

type *h* = **array** [1..5] **of** *integer*;

A way of partially overcoming the difficulty of writing array manipulatin procedures which can be used generally for arrays of different size (provide they have the same number of dimensions), is to use a constant when specifyin the array type, for example:

const *n* = 5;
type *arraytype* 1 = **array** [1..*n*] **of** *integer*;
procedure *arrayproc* (*g* : *arraytype* 1);

The only program change needed, in order to deal with different sized array of similar dimension is to change the definition of the constant *n*.

But the same procedure or function cannot be used for manipulation o different sized arrays in the same program, and this is considered to be a desig error in the Pascal language which greatly reduces its value for real computin concerned with matrix calculations. This feature of Pascal is not commonl found in other high-level programming languages.

15.2 PARAMETERS OF TYPE function OR procedure

A procedure or function parameter, as we have seen, can be a value or variabl of any type, for example *char, boolean, integer, real, array, pointer,* or *recor* But we may wish to pass as parameter neither a value nor a variable, but function or procedure, and Pascal allows this provided it is specified in th procedure or function heading, for example:

function *x* (**function** *f* : *real*) : *real*;

function *y* (**procedure** *p*) : *real*;

procedure *s* (**procedure** *p*);

procedure *t* (**function** *g* : *real*);

This can be a most useful facility, an example of its use being in the nume cal calculation of definite integrals.

15.2.1 Calculation of a definite integral

The definite integral:

$$I = \int_a^b f(x)\,dx$$

is the function of three variables:

$$I = I(f, a, b)$$

where f is of type function, and a and b are of type *real*. If the integral is to be calculated numerically, this amounts to saying it will be approximated by a summation of some kind, and if we denote the number of terms in the sum by n, then:

$$I = I(f, a, b, n)$$

An appropriate function heading for a Pascal integration function reflects the fact that I is a function of these four arguments:

function I(**function** f : *real*, *lwb*, *upb* : *real*; n : *integer*) : *real*;

{f is the integrand, a function of one variable; *lwb*, *upb* are lower bound and upper bound, n is the number of values summed}

For maximum simplicity, we shall use the very rough approximation:

$$I = h * \Sigma \{f(k*h + lwb)\}$$

where $h = (upb - lwb)/n$, and the summation is for $k = 1$ to n.

The function f can of course be any integrand. As an example we shall take:

$$f = \sqrt{(r^2 - x^2)}$$
$$lwb = 0$$
$$upb = r$$

so that the integral is the area of a quarter-circle of radius r. The two function declarations required are as follows:

```
function Integrate (function f : real; lwb, upb : real; n : integer) : real;
var sum, h : real; k : integer;
    begin
        h := (upb - lwb)/n;
        sum := 0;
            for k := 1 to n do
                sum := sum + f(h*k + lwb);
            I := sum*h
    end;
```

```
function y (x : real) : real;
   begin
      y := sqrt(r*r − x*x)
   end {of function Integrate};
```

With $n = 10$, a program statement to calculate and print the value of the area of the circle, radius r would be:

$$write(4*Integrate(y, 0, r, n));$$

which gives an approximation to:

$$4\int_0^r \sqrt{(r^2 - x^2)}\,\mathrm{d}x$$

that is,

$$4*h*\Sigma\{\sqrt{(r^2 - (h*k)^2)}\}$$

where

$h = r/n$ and the summation is for $k = 1$ to n.

However, the function *Integrate* may be used to integrate *any* integrand. All that is required is to call *Integrate*, using as actual parameters the appropriate integrand function, and appropriate lower and upper bounds.

EXAMPLES:

(i) for $\displaystyle\int_0^1 sin(x)\mathrm{d}x$ use:

   $$Integrate(sin, 0, 1, 10)$$

   or for greater accuracy:

   $$Integrate(sin, 0, 1, 20)$$

(ii) for $\displaystyle\int_{100}^{200} x^2\,\mathrm{d}x$ use:

   $$Integrate(sqr, 100, 200, 10)$$

   for $\displaystyle\int_0^3 \sqrt{x}\,\mathrm{d}x$ use:

   $$Integrate(sqrt, 0, 3, 10)$$

To calculate any single integral, two functions are required:

(i) A summation (that is, numerical integration) function, declared using a function identical in form to that of *Integrate*, with four parameters like those of *Integrate*. The algorithm used to approximate the integration can however be vastly improved. The trapezoidal formula, Simpson's rule, or a Gaussian integration formula may be used, (see Section 15.3).

(ii) A function is required to evaluate the integrand, and, unless it happens to be a standard function, must itself be declared, and will generally take the same form of function heading as the function y.

15.2.2 Double or multiple integrals

In the case of a multiple integral, the same integration function as that for a single integral can be used without modification. However, a trick is needed with the integrand. The integrand of a multiple integration (say of multiplicity M) is of course a function of M variables, for example:

$$g(x1, x2, x3, \ldots, xM)$$

But a parametric function of only one variable, say $g1$, must be declared, and defined so that:

$$g1(p) = g(p, x2, x3, \ldots, xM)$$

thus enabling g to be evaluated by direct call of $g1$ from the integrating function.

As an example, we take the double integral for the volume of a sphere of radius r.

15.2.3 Example of a double-integration

The volume of a half-sphere is found by integrating along the z-axis, summing together all the disc-shaped slices perpendicular to it. The radius of each disc is a function of z. It varies from r, at $z = 0$, to 0, at $z = r$, and is given by the expression:

$$\sqrt{(r^2 - z^2)}$$

so the integral giving the volume of the half-sphere is computed by the expression:

Integrate$(discarea, 0, \sqrt{(r*r - z*z)}, n)$

where n is the number of points.

We shall need a function *discarea* which is passed as a parameter to *Integrate*, and which, when called, returns the value computed for the area of a disc. It does this by itself calling *Integrate*, and passing to it as parameters the function y and the integration limits to be used. The appropriate expression is therefore:

$4*Integrate(y, 0, upperlimit, n)$

where, this time, *upperlimit* $= \sqrt{(r^2 - x^2 - z^2)}$, which gives the area of one quadrant, and so we multiply the integral by 4.

The function *y*, passed as a parameter in the call of *Integrate* made within *discarea* is very similar to the function *y* declared in Section 15.2.1, except that since we have introduced a third dimension, *z*, in addition to *x* and *y*, the mathematical form of *y* is now:

$$y = \sqrt{(r^2 - x^2 - z^2)}$$

However, as explained in Section 15.2.2, we treat *y* as a function of the single variable, *x*, because *r* an *z* are constants during each integration of *y*. The variable *r* is declared globally and its value remains unchanged during the entire integration. However, the value of *z* is computed anew within *Integrate*, for each call of *discarea*. This value is outside the scope of the function *y* and so, inside *discarea*, we copy it to a global variable *z* which can be accessed from within *y*.

A complete program for finding the volume of a sphere follows. Within function *discarea*, the formal parameter has been called *zz* to call attention to the fact that *discarea* is defined as a function of *zz* alone, *r* and *x* being global constants. Similarly, within the function *y*, the formal parameter has been called *xx*, to distinguish it from *r* and *z* for similar reasons. An even more important reason is to prevent the global variable *z* being made *inaccessible* (see Section 10.1.1).

```
program sphere(output);
var halfsphere, r, pi, z : real;
    n : integer;
    function integrate(function f : real; lwb, upb : real; n : integer) : real;
    var dummy, h, sum : real;
       begin
           h := (upb − lwb)/n;
           sum := 0;
             for k := 1 to n do
                 sum := sum + f(h∗k + lwb);
             integrate := h∗sum
       end {of function integrate};
    function y(xx : real) : real;
    var val : real;
       begin
           val := r∗r − xx∗xx − z∗z;
           {now make sure that val is not negative, as it might be, due to
           rounding error when nearly zero, before taking square root}
              if (val > 0)
              then val := sqrt(val)
              else val := 0,
```

```
    y := val
  end {of function y};
function discarea(zz : real) : real;
var dummy : real;
  begin
    dummy := r*r − zz*zz;
    {when zz is nearly equal to r, rounding error could make dummy
    negative, and as we are going to take the square root, we avoid
    trouble by the following statement}
      if dummy > 0
      then dummy := sqrt(dummy)
      else dummy := 0;
    {and now, before calling Integrate, the current value of zz, whose
    scope is local to discarea, must be made accessible within the function y,
    which uses it. We do this by copying zz to the global variable z}
    z := zz;
    discarea := 4*Integrate(y, 0, dummy, n)
  end {of function discarea};
begin {main program}
  pi := 4*arctan(1);
  {this is an easy way of getting an accurate value of pi without the
  risk of making copying errors}
  n := 20 {number of points};
  r := exp(ln(0.75/pi)/3);
  {setting r equal to the cube root of (0.75/pi) is a good test value since
  it should result in the volume of the sphere being equal to 1}
  writeln(' expected volume of sphere =', 4*pi*r*r*r/3);
  halfsphere := Integrate(discarea, 0, r, n);
  writeln(' calculated volume of sphere = ', 2*halfsphere);
  writeln(' using', n, ' point integration')
end.
```

5.3 USING AN EFFICIENT METHOD OF INTEGRATION

his is a brief note on three well-known algorithms for numerical approximation
f integrals. They are the trapezoidal rule, Simpson's formula, and Gaussian
itegration. For brevity we shall refer to them by I, S and G respectively.

References to works giving theoretical treatment and explanation may be
ound in the bibliographic index. What follows is a description of each method
nd a guide to which method to use. In each case, the formula given is an
pproximation to the value of the integral:

$$\int_a^b f(x)\,\mathrm{d}x$$

15.3.1 Trapezoidal rule

The interval $(b - a)$ is divided into n equal parts of length $h = (b - a)/n$, and the formula is given by:

$$0.5*h\{f(b) + f(a)\} + h* \sum_{k=1}^{n-1} \{f(a + k*h)\}$$

The theoretical estimate of error, using the trapezoidal rule, is given by:

$$e = h^2[f'(b) - f'(a)]/12$$

that is, it is proportional to the square of the interval h, and it is proportional to the difference in slope of the function $f(x)$ at the two end points a and b.

15.3.2 Simpson's rule

The interval $(b - a)$ *must* be divided into an *even* number of sub-intervals, say $n = 2*j$, each sub-interval being of length $h = (b - a)/n$.

$$S = (2*h/3)*\{0.5*(f(a) + f(b)) + \sum_{k=1}^{n-1} \{(k \bmod 2 + 1)*f(a + k*h)\}\}$$

The theoretical estimate of error using Simpson's rule is given by:

$$e = h^4[f'''(b) - f'''(a)]/180$$

that is, it is proportional to the fourth power of the interval h, and it is proportional to the difference in the third derivatives of the function $f(x)$ at the two end points a and b. Notice also the improvement in the proportionality factor, 180, as compared with 12 in the trapezoidal rule.

15.3.3 Gaussian integration

This method gives an *estimated* error approximately the same as Simpson, when using only *half* as many points. In addition, the actual error is often very much smaller. Its disadvantage arises only if the function to be integrated has been given as equally-spaced tabular values, since it requires its points at certain selected unequal intervals. This is no disadvantage if the function values have in any case to be calculated.

Gaussian integration formulas take the form:

$$G(n) = \sum_{k=1}^{n} W_k*f(X_k), \qquad -1 \leqslant X \leqslant 1,$$

where the values of the X_k and W_k depend upon certain properties of the Legendre polynomials. These important mathematical functions have long been well tabulated, so the values required may be obtained from the published table (see bibliographic index). The X_k are the values of X for which the Legendre polynomials are zero, and are called the zeroes of the polynomials, while the W are called weighting coefficients, or weights.

Use of this method requires that the limits of integration shall be from -1 o $+1$, and this normalisation is easily achieved by a transformation of the riginal variable x, whose interval is (a, b) to the new variable X whose interval s $(-1, +1)$.

The transformations required are:

$$x = m*X + c$$

vhere

$$m = (b - a)/2$$

.nd

$$c = (a + b)/2$$

$$dx = m*dX$$

The integration formula then becomes:

$$G(n) = m* \sum_{k=1}^{n} W_k*f(m*X_k + c)$$

For $n = 5$, the values of X_k and W_k are as follows:

k	X_k	W_k
1	0.0	0.5688888889
2	0.5384693101	0.4786286705
3	-0.5384693101	0.4786286705
4	0.9061798459	0.2369268851
5	-0.9061798459	0.2369268851

15.3.4 A trapezoidal integration function

```
function trapezintegrate (function f : real; lwb, upb : real; n : integer) : real;
var sum, h : real; k : integer;
   begin
      h := (upb − lwb)/n;
      sum := 0.5*(f(upb) + f(lwb));
         for k := 1 to n − 1 do
            sum := sum + f(lwb + k*h);
         trapezintegrate := h*sum
   end;
```

15.3.5 A Simpson integration function

```
function Simpson (function f : real; lwb, upb : real; n : integer) : real;
var sum, h : real; j : integer;
   begin
      if odd(n) then n := n + 1;
```

```
        h := (upb − lwb)/n;
        sum := 0.5*(f(lwb) + f(upb));
     for j := 1 to n − 1 do
        sum := sum + (j mod 2 + 1)*f(lwb + j*h);
     Simpson := 2*h*sum/3
     end {of function Simpson};
```

15.3.6 A Gaussian integration function

```
function Gaussint5 (function f : real; lwb, upb : real) : real;
type C = array [1..5] of real;
var W, Z, x : C; r, s, sum : real; k : integer;
   begin
      W[1] := 0.5688888889; Z[1] := 0.0;
      W[2] := 0.4786286705; Z[2] := 0.5384693101;
      W[3] := W[2];          Z[3] := −Z[2];
      W[4] := 0.2369268851; Z[4] := 0.9061798459;
      W[5] := W[4];          Z[5] := −Z[4];
      {W and Z are weights and zeroes}
      r := (upb − lwb)/2;
      s := (upb + lwb)/2;
      {normalisation constants}
        for k := 1 to 5 do
           begin
              x[k] := r*Z[k] + s;
              sum := sum + W[k]*f(x[k])
           end;
        Gaussint5 := r*sum
   end;
```

15.4 PROBLEMS

15.4.1

Write a two-parameter procedure which changes the values of two real variable say x and y, so that the new values are $(x + y)$ and $(x − y)$ respectively.

15.4.2

Modify **program** *sphere* in Section 15.2.2 by incorporating the function *trapezintegrate*, *Simpson*, and *Gaussint5*. Use the program to calculate th volume using each of the four methods in turn, with $n = 10$ for *integrate* *trapezintegrate*, and *Simson*, but $n = 5$ for *Gaussint5*. Print out the value an error for each result.

5.4.3

Calculate the integral of *sin*(x) between $x = 0$ and $x = pi/2$ using the trapezoidal rule, Simson's rule, Gaussian integration. Print all 3 results and their differences from the expected result as found by using $\cos(x)$.

CHAPTER 16

How to be a good programmer

'Where do you come from?' said the Red Queen, 'and where are you going?
Look up, speak nicely, and don't twiddle your fingers all the time'.

Lewis Carroll

There is a story of a very earnest student who approached a very earnest professor and engaged in the following conversation. 'I have read and re-read all
your textbooks, I have committed your brief lecture notes to memory, I have
written an essay upon the main aspect of each of your lectures. I have worked
solutions to all the problems set in your textbooks, and I have followed up and
studied carefully all the references you gave. What can I do,' asked the student,
'to improve my knowledge?' The professor replied immediately and with
enthusiasm – 'Even more!'

What is programming skill? In this broadest sense, programming includes
many stages in a long process, the logical order of whose steps is as follows:

  (i) Vague formulation of a problem.
 (ii) Identification and clear specification of the true problem (which may
       be quite different from the original formulation).
(iii) Choice of a method of solution, that is an algorithmic method.
 (iv) Design and specification of the algorithm to be used.
  (v) Design and specification of the data structures to be used.
 (vi) Choice of suitable programming language.
(vii) First level specification of the program, that is a refinement of (iv)
       which is dependent on (v) and (vi).
(viii) Step by step development and testing of modules of the program,
       fitting them together to constitute the program.
 (ix) Field testing of the program as a whole, using data designed to try to
       make the program fail.

There are various narrower interpretations of the role of the programmer.
Stages (i) and (ii) are frequently considered to be the job of a systems analyst,
and sometimes this job extends to stages further down the list. There are no
universal divisions, but the subject matter of this book is concerned mainly with
stages (iv), (v), (vii), (viii) and (ix), not by any means because the other stages
are either unimportant or without interest, but because they merit books to
themselves, and there is no suggestion that they may be ignored.

Dividing the task of programming into a number of sequential stages is itself of some importance. The programmer who is not fully aware of the necessary function of each stage may well fail to produce satisfactory programs.

16.1 THIS PROGRAM IS FINE, BUT IT'S NOT WHAT WE NEEDED!

In fact, the programmer who tries to skip stage (ii) does so at his peril. The result of failing to produce (or obtain from his client or systems analyst) a clear specification of the problem, may be, and very often *is*, that a very nice program is produced, which however, unfortunately, does something quite different from what is required.

16.2 CHOOSING YOUR ALGORITHMIC METHOD

Stage (iii) is equally important. Bad choice of algorithmic method, often through failure to investigate thoroughly the choice of standard methods available, leads to wasted effort and wasted computer resource. Sometimes, not only is the wrong method chosen, but, using the right method, programs already exist (and are often available in program libraries) which will do the job required. Choice of algorithmic method is worth at least a small example.

PROBLEM:

To compute the value of the sum of the first n integers, where n has a large value, say 100 000. One method is so obvious and simple that real thought is hastily brushed aside by producing a program such as:

```
program sumintegers1 (input, output);
var k, n, sum : integer;
   begin
     read (n);
     write (' sum of the first', n, 'integers = ');
     sum := 0;
        for k := 1 to n do
           sum := sum + k;
           writeln (sum)
   end.
```

Is this a good program? Yes, but the algorithmic method stinks! If n has the value 100 000, this program will take (approximately) 100 000 instructions to run to completion. It so happens that the value of the sum required is equal to $n(n + 1)/2$ (the proof is left to the reader).

Using this formula, a new version *sumintegers2* can be written which takes only two instructions, regardless of the numerical value of n:

```
program sumintegers2 (input, output);
var n : integer;
```

```
begin
    read(n);
    writeln(' sum of first', n, 'integers = ', n*(n + 1)/2)
end.
```

16.3 PROGRAM DESIGN

This embraces two important stages. The first is specification of the algorithm and the second is specification of the data structures to be used.

Design and specification of algorithm is not the same as choice of algorithmic method. The method may be denoted simply by a name, for example Newton's method of iterative approximation, binary search, use of Chebyshev series, etc. Sometimes, the algorithmic method amounts to little more than recognition and specification of the tasks to be carried out and the constraints to be observed. Design of the algorithm is more detailed, and entails the linking together of these tasks in a logical order. The first version of the **program** *noughtsandcrosses*, in Section 9.4, was a simple example of the specification of an algorithm. The essential feature of this exercise is that the algorithm is being designed at a level which is as detailed as it can be *while still remaining independent of* choice of *data structures*. A common error made by programmers is to pre-empt this stage of algorithm design by an immediate choice of data structure beforehand. This not only restricts the choice of algorithm but, much worse, it confuses it by introducing detail which is irrelevant at this stage and makes the design more difficult. The result of doing this is likely to be that you cannot see the wood for the trees — you cannot concentrate upon the principal design features, because you become trapped in the maze of detail associated with particular data structures. Stand back and you will see the full picture.

Designing the algorithm results in the production of a pseudo-program consisting largely of comments, as in Section 9.4, and this level of program specification is a vital part of program documentation (of which more will be said later). This version of the algorithm (program) is often specified in the form of a flow chart. Used in this way, a flow chart can be effectively informative and a help in checking the logical structure of the algorithm. (This stage in algorithm design is rather like a well formulated plan for writing an essay, consisting of a note or heading for each section or paragraph of the essay).

The result of producing this design for an algorithm is that it implicitly points to the kind of operations we shall want to carry out upon the data, to the relationships between data items we want to make clear and the types of data we want to build into the data structures we choose; and this is the firm basis upon which we consider and choose how to organise our data, choose meaningful names as far as possible for the main variables and constants we require, and write out their description together with comments explaining their role in the context of the algorithmic design already produced.

16.4 CHOICE OF PROGRAMMING LANGUAGE

To the student this may seem strange, because the choice of language has been made before he begins, but with a real-life programming project of any size, it is only after a substantial amount of program design work has been done, as already described, that it becomes possible to make a sensible choice of language The reason for this is that different languages offer different facilities for the structuring and manipulation of data.

Proper choice of language for a particular project is therefore not merely a matter of personal preference, nor of the idiosyncrasies of the syntax of different languages. The main reason Pascal has been chosen for this book is that it provides all the data structures and operations required in an introductory course on programming, as well as providing clear and powerful language struc tues such as blocks, loop structures, function or procedure structures, and the choice of passing parameters by value or by name.

Clearly, the data structures provided in a language affect the detailed methods to be used in the refinement of the algorithm, while the language struc tures available affect the ease and clarity with which those methods may be expressed and defined.

16.5 STEP BY STEP REFINEMENT – SPECIFICATION AT A MORE   DETAILED LEVEL

At this stage, an important step forward can be taken. The algorithm can be given the form of a program, say in Pascal. The main declarations can be written and the algorithm, already defined but as yet expressed in a way independent of the data structures since chosen, may now be expressed in terms of these struc tures, but still at a high level of generality without descending to a mass of detail.

This refinement results in a structure for the program clearly emerging with particular modules of program standing by themselves, as tasks which can be tackled separately.

In the case of a large project, this is the stage at which a project leader might assign the further development of particular modules to particular pro grammers who are members of his team. But before doing so, each module must have its interface with the program as a whole defined. What is meant by interface?

A module may be a function or procedure. If so, then the rudiments of the interface are contained in the information given in the function or procedure heading. This information is incomplete however. It must be supplemented by a list of the names and types of all the global variables which may be referred to within the module. In addition, brief but clear comments must be added describing the role of each of these variables, and of each of the parameters and, most inportant of all, a list of those global variables whose values can become *changed* by the action of the statements within the module.

It should be clear that the specification of the algorithm to be implemented by the module is subject to a similar process of design and refinement as applies to the whole program. This process leads to a further level of refinement, and continues until we get down to actual programming statements (that is, Pascal instructions). This iterative process is called *step-by-step refinement*.

The order in which modules are selected for refinement and development into sub-programs (or program fragments) can be very important. What is important is to select first a module which can be tested (by a suitable short program) independently of the other modules. This means selecting a module which does not make use of other modules. When it is tested and apparently working, further modules which use it may be developed and tested. So, piece by piece, the program is constructed by the joining together of prefabricated and pretested modules.

16.6 TESTING WORKING PROGRAMS

16.6.1 Is the program correct?

Choosing data with which to test a program calls for the exercise of skill and of ordinary everyday common-sense. Of course it is easier to devise *many* tests, and test one thing at a time, and more sensible to do so, because then any failure will pin-point the area of the error.

(i) Choose data such that you either know or can easily calculate the correct answer by hand, with minimal effort. For example, if the program is to solve a quadratic equation, choose the roots first, choose them to be small integer values, and then calculate the values of the coefficients of the equation to be solved. These coefficients constitute the test data for testing the program (at least for one test).

(ii) Look for special values of data which could prove sensitive to the program. For example, with the quadratic program, choose a pair of real roots, a pair of coincident roots, a pair of complex roots, a pair of roots with one root zero, and a pair of roots both zero.

(iii) The idea behind choosing test data is to try to make the program fail, not to show that it works, to try to show that it can produce wrong answers, not to see that it may sometimes produce correct ones. Choose the data accordingly. Quite frequently zero is a sensitive data value, and sometimes so are negative values. End values at the extremes of a range of some kind can be useful. Another useful trick is to choose data which leaves the program nothing to do. For example, how will a sorting program behave if presented with data which is already sorted, or with no data at all? Sometimes, having nothing to do will make a program go wrong.

16.6.2 Is the program robust?

What is meant by program robustness? It means loosely speaking that the program will stand up to rough treatment without falling down. Take any program, and try to think of a way of making it fail, for example, by feeding it incorrect data. If the program gives you an error message, then it is a robust program. If instead it fails, and the computer system gives you an error message, that program was not so robust.

Robustness is an important quality which is desirable in any program. In a program written for use by a number of other people it is essential. This applies particularly to programs to be included in program libraries.

There are of course degrees of robustness, and practical compromise is sometimes made between checking for every possible misuse on the one hand, and breaking down at *any* misuse on the other. In the case of functions or procedures whose actual parameters may be calculated by program at run-time, it may be desirable sometimes to safeguard against disasters by testing, but there is not much point in having a built-in test in the program if there is no remedy. Sometimes a test and a remedy can be devised. For example, a calculation might cause overflow during evaluation of an intermediate result, though not in the final result. In such a case it is often possible to change the order of the calculation, or to make the intermediate calculation some other way, such as using logarithms, in order to reduce the magnitude of the quantities involved in the sensitive operations.

Part of the exercise of testing a program should be to devise conditions under which the program will break down. What implicit assumptions are made by the program? – ignore them, and break it! Then set about modifying it to make it more robust.

16.7 THERE'S NOTHING WRONG WITH MY PROGRAM, SO WHY DOESN'T IT WORK?

This section is about bugs. Bugs have an interesting history. At one time they were considered to be nothing but a pestilence rightly inflicted upon the lazy, dirty and undeserving poor. Later, with the spread of scientific enlightenment, they were recognised as creatures of profound interest to the biologist. But technological advance changed all that, and when the impetus of the second world war brought us such mind-boggling wonders as television, radar, and electronics, it was discovered that all the new wizard equipment was inhabited by bugs – little demonaic creatures which could not be seen with the naked eye – malevolent creatures whose sole purpose and delight it was to make the equipment go wrong, and in such a way as to defy diagnosis.

When computers were invented, these second generation bugs thought they had it made for them, and entered with zest into computer hardware. But the worst was yet to come. A satanic mutation was no doubt responsible for the ew third generation bugs who live in computer software. Some people believe that programmers in fact spend most of their time in getting bugs out of their programs.

It is well known that the way to deal with biological bugs is to have a good bath, and to continue the treatment with regular and ample doses of soap and hot water. Furthermore, it is held that if you keep clean in the first place, you will not be attacked by bugs anyway. Similar considerations have been applied to programs. Bugs love to inhabit programs which are large, full of narrow twisting passages along which program control flows in a bewildering maze, even many passages through which control never flows at all, thus allowing dirt to accumulate and bugs to breed, and they love the dark. Simple sparkling programs, well lit by the disciplined use of uncomplicated structures and illuminating comment seem to keep them away, at least except for the stray intruder who is easily spotted and quickly dealt with.

Hence the importance of step-by-step development of a program in small well-defined modules which are simple, clean even to the point of elegance, and easily tested. Hence the importance of fitting these modules together step-by-step, adding one at a time, and keeping the bugs out. Keeping the bugs out of programs is done by disciplined attention to routine checking of detail at the preparation stage, not by the exercise of fiendish skill in outwitting the bugs.

Even at the most trivial level, developing the habit of automatically checking that there is a semicolon separating every pair of statements is a part of such discipline. Note: the time to do that particular check is immediately after every occurrence of **end** when you are writing a program – in other words, as soon as you finish writing a compound statement. Another example at this level is that when you have finished writing the program, go through it and methodically list all the identifiers used. Then check this list against your declarations and definitions.

At a less trivial level, examine every loop in the program, and, for each one, write down the conditions which must be satisfied:

(i) for the loop to be entered;

(ii) for the loop to be continued;

(iii) for exit from the loop to occur.

Having done this, do a trace table which shows the value of all relevant variables immediately before entering the loop and after once or twice traversing the loop. Do another trace table to cover the state immediately before and after the last time of traversing the loop. This exercise is getting very close to something which the experts call proof of program correctness, currently one of the many rich fields of research in computer science.

Keeping your programs clean will keep most of the bugs away, but not all. Programs are devised and written by human beings, and one human characteristic is to err. So we still have to tackle the problem, not of how to keep the bugs away, but of how to get them out once they are in.

In this endeavour, the concept of the trace table is invaluable. For smal
simple pieces of program, a trace table can be constructed by hand; but ver)
often the detail entailed by such a task is too great. Here we must harness th(
computer to do the tedious and detailed work for us. How can we do that"
Consider a small simple program as a silly example. It is not difficult to devis(
write statements to be inserted after every statement in the program which
changes the value of any variable. These inserted *write* statements would produc(
exactly the entries that must be made in a trace table. We could go furthe)
and, by full use of the sophisticated facilities available for control of layou(
in *write* statements, insert further statements so that the modified progran
actually outputs its own complete trace table. Although this is neither necessary
nor the most useful thing to *do*, it is one of the most important things to *understand*, because this idea can be harnessed as a powerful warhorse in the battle tc
diagnose an unexplained bug.

For a large program, or for any program containing any loops which ar(
traversed a large number of times, the printed output of a complete trace tabl(
would be enormous. For almost any non-trivial program, it would be too larg(
to be really useful. We do not actually want to look at the *whole* of such a table
What we should like to do is to look at selected parts of it. For example, in th(
case of a program which aborts with a runtime error, we should certainly lik(
to see the trace table as it stood just before aborting. This would show which
value in which variable was responsible for the runtime error. We could the)
make further selections of points of time in the program at which we should lik(
to see the trace table. In a different case we could make our selections basically
in pairs, giving us pairs of photo-flashes of the state of the program − the first o
each pair occurring before the error, and the second after if (that is, if the abort
though caused by the error, occurred some time after it). Our first pair might b(
widely spaced, the important thing being to make sure we have trapped th(
error between them. Subsequent pairs of photo-flashes would be closer togethe)
each selection bracketing the error between closer and closer points in th(
program. When the brackets enclose only one program statement we hav(
located the error.

We obtain these pairs of photo-flash views of the runtime state of th(
program by inserting appropriate *write* statements, not at *every* point in th(
program, but at our carefully selected crucial points. If we make immediat(
guesses as to the exact source of trouble we may miss. In the long run, it i)
better to cast the net widely and narrow the gap systematically. As it narrows
we often change the write statements, to give more information about som(
variables, less about others. We are narrowing our view of the trace table no(
only to a particular few rows, that is a particular time interval, but also to :
particular few columns, that is to the change in value of certain crucial variables
The technique to be employed is rather like that used in binary search (see
where at each examination we try to halve the interval which contains what w(

re looking for. If we do this, the interval becomes small very quickly, and we ave reduced the problem of looking for a needle in a haystack to the simpler ne of picking it up, having located it.

6.8 PROGRAMMING EFFICIENCY

Wasteful use of computing resources can be expensive without any worthwhile return for the outlay. Care in avoiding it brings a certain satisfaction and even adds elegance to a program.

Consider the following program, which reads in values for n and x, and then calculates the value of the summation for $k = 1$ to n of:

$$\Sigma\{(2k-1)\sin(x) + \cos(x)\}(k!)/(2k-1)$$

```
program wilfulwaste(input, output);
function factorial(r : integer) : integer;
var j, f : integer;
  begin
    f := 1;
      if r > 1
      then for j := 1 to r do f := f*j;
    factorial := f
  end;
var k, n : integer; x, sum : real;
  begin
    read(x, n);
    writeln(' for n = ', n, 'and x = ', x);
    sum := 0;
      for k := 1 to n do
        sum := sum + ((2*k − 1)*sin(x) + cos(x))*
                    factorial(n)/(2*k − 1);
    writeln(' sum = ', sum)
  end.
```

From many aspects, this is a good program. It has clarity and simplicity. It is easy to read and check, and it even has some robustness (consider what happens if n is negative). But it is grossly inefficient and wasteful of computer time. Let us consider ways of cutting out some of the waste. Points to look for and take action on are as follows:

(i) Never perform within a loop, many times, an operation which produces the same result and could therefore be performed once only, outside the loop and used as a constant within it. The more expensive the operation, the more important is this point; and it applies in this case to the evaluation of the sub-expressions $sin(x)$ and $cos(x)$.

(ii) Never calculate twice or more times, a value which can be calculate● once and stored. This applies to the evaluation of the sub-expressio● $(2*k-1)$.

(iii) When using a loop to calculate the sum of a series of terms, it is fre● quently possible to save much time by calculating each term startin● with the preceding term rather than starting from scratch. This poin● applies to the evaluation of *factorial*(k).

(iv) The overheads in machine-time associated with procedure entry an● exit may be relatively high if the actual work done in the body of th● procedure is small. In this case it is more efficient to include the cod● of the procedure body directly within the loop from which the pro● cedure is called in place of the procedure call itself.

A more efficient version of *wilfulwaste* follows, after a closer look at th● expression to be evaluated. If we separate the two terms, we can move th● $sin(x)$ and $cos(x)$ terms outside the summations as factors to give:

$$sin(x)\Sigma(k!) + cos(x)\Sigma(k!)/(2k-1)$$

```
program frugal(input, output);
var sum1, sum2, sum, x : real;
    k, f, n : integer;
  begin
    read(x, n);
    writeln(' x =', x, 'and n =', n);
    sum1 := 0; sum2 := 0; f := 1;
      for k := 1 to n do
        begin
          f := f*k;
          sum1 := sum1 + f;
          sum2 := sum2 + f/(2*k-1)
        end;
        sum := sum1*sin(x) + sum2*cos(x);
      writeln('sum = ', sum)
end.
```

There is one general point which must be made with regard to efficiency:

Be efficient where it is effective.

When seeking to improve the machine-time effficiency of a program it is important to consider the sections of the program which take up relatively much time. To halve the runtime of a section which accounts for only one per cent of the total run-time is not very effective compared to halving the run-time of a section which accounts for, say, fifty per cent of the total run time.

Most of the time spent by all programs is in loops. Even more time is spent in loops within loops. A loop within a loop may not be obvious; the inner loop may occur within the body of a procedure call inside the outer loop.

It must be recognised, however, that the cost of a program which will be used for a long period includes its cost of maintenance, occasional modification, and sometimes transfer (to a new machine or a new compiler). This cost consists partly of human programming effort, including human maintenance programming, often by someone who did not write the program, and when the original programmer has long since moved on to new pastures.

Programs nearly always need modifications, especially if they are used again some time after their first being used. After an elapse of time, even if the original programmer is still around, he has probably forgotten all the details he had in mind when originally writing the program.

Modification of an existing program can take many hours longer than it should if the program lacks simplicity and clarity. If, in addition to being complicated and difficult to understand, the program has no useful documentation, it is often easier to start again and write a new program.

16.9 SIMPLICITY, CLARITY AND GOOD DOCUMENTATION

Those are the hallmarks of the work of a good programmer. When they die, programmers who have left behind them programs which are simple, clear and well-documented go to heaven. The others, if there is eternal justice, suffer the hell of trying to unravel the mysteries of their own and each others' programs.

Documentation alone is not enough, it must be useful documentation. It is bad enough trying to understand the complexities of a twisted and tangled program. Insult is added in injury if one is obliged in addition to wade through a mass of unintelligible documentation, which appears to have been provided for no good reason other than evidence of the information explosion.

Program documentation can be divided into two parts: one part is embedded in and along with the program, in the form of comments, and in the names chosen for identifiers, while the other part is quite separate from the program itself. A program which contains good documentary comments embedded in it is sometimes called a self-documenting program. It is good practice to embed documentation in this way, for the following reasons:

(i) Sometimes the separated documentation gets lost, not necessarily completely lost, but lost enough so that the person who needs it does not get it, or perhaps is unaware that it exists.

(ii) Embedded comments can be placed at exactly the postion in the program where they are relevant and will be read at the time they are relevant.

(iii) By having the comments embedded in the program, they are more likely to be changed when they ought to be, at any time when the program has been changed. Otherwise when a program is modified, the documentation may easily be forgotten and not brought up to date.

Wherever the documentation exists and however it is organised, it should include the following:

1. A short statement of the purpose of the program.
2. An explanation of any mathematical methods, and details of any formulas used, or references to such information.
3. A clear concise explanation to a potential user of how to go about using the program. This is really a description of the program interface. It should include details of the compiler and operating system under which the program runs, the external files, program libraries, subroutines used by it, the job control commands necessary to run it, a sample of input data and corresponding output, and full details of the required format and nature of the input data. It should also give some guidance as to the program's requirements of computing resources such as time, storage, and lines or pages of output.
4. A specification of the algorithm which the program purports to implement. This specification should be at the level described in Section 16.3.
5. A list of all the variables used in the program, describing the type of each and the purpose for which it is used.
6. A specification for each program module (function or procedure), which includes a definition of its interface as described in Section 16.5, and also includes sections corresponding to 1, 2 and 4 of this list.
7. A complete listing of the program.
8. Identity of the author, and date and version identification of the program. This section should provide space for later notes containing a reference to each modification made later to the program.

As pointed out earlier, as much as possible of the details of documentation should be embedded in the program in the form of comments. One such comment should refer to the existence of the separate documentation and say how access to it may be obtained.

16.10 PROBLEMS

16.10.1

Consider an algorithm to calculate and print the value of the first 10 000 primes. Write a discursive description which explains your step by step development and improvement of the algorithm. Keep your discussion independent of program language and data structures. Assume you are to be paid a fixed fee for your program design work, and that you must pay for the computer time required to run the resulting program, out of your fixed fee.

16.10.2

Produce full documentation for a program which will follow the design followed in Problem 16.10.1. (The program is not required).

16.10.3

If you had no time to do any programming yourself, but three programmers were available, and a deadline to meet, how would you divide among them the work of writing and testing the required program of 16.10.1.

16.10.4

Examine each of the programs you have written in answer to problems set at the ends of previous chapters, and devise data which is not illegal, but which will *break* the program.

Reading list

This is a short list giving the author's personal preferences for books which signpost the way in various directions for further reading. They are not arranged in an order corresponding to the chapters of this book, because there is so much overlap, but under headings descriptive of their content.

COMPUTERS FROM THE INSIDE

BARTREE, THOMAS C. (1972), *Digital Computer Fundamentals*, McGraw-Hill.

The nitty gritty of computers. The use of digital electronics and logical circuits in the design of computer memories, processor units and peripheral devices. Clear and detailed explanations of the implementation of binary arithmetic and other machine level operations.

COMPUTERS FROM THE OUTSIDE

MEEK, BRIAN L. and FAIRTHORNE, SIMON (1977), *Using Computers*, Ellis Horwood.

This kaleidoscopic introduction to all aspects of computers and computing is an excellent beginners book which does not overwhelm with too many technical details.

NEUMANN, JOHN VON, *The Computer and the Brain*, (1974), Yale University Press.

Written in 1956 by a truly great mathematician shortly before his early and tragic death, this thought provoking essay is still highly relevant.

GENERAL

CARROLL, LEWIS (1865), *Alice Through the Looking Glass*.

Mistakenly thought to be for children, but actually essential reading for adults who are interested in the use of logic and language.

NUMERICAL COMPUTATION

GROVE, WENDELL E. (1966), *Brief Numerical Methods*, Prentice-Hall.

A highly informative handbook, especially useful for the non-speciali
who wants to know which methods to use for his numerical application
as well as how to use them.

PROBLEM SOLVING

POLYA, G. (1957), *How to solve it*, Open University Press.

A pocket study of the rules of discovery and invention, their history an
knowhow. It raises the art of problem solving to the level of a science.

PROGRAMMING

MAURER, WARD DOUGLAS (1968). *Programming, an introduction to com
puter languages and techniques*, Holden-Day.

Starts right in with machine language — the language into which any othe
computer language must be translated in order to run on a computer. It
about programming, not about any particular language.

WIRTH, NICKLAUS (1976), *Algorithms + Data Structures = Programs*, Prentice
Hall.

Recommended as the book to continue with after this one, if you want t
know more about the basic concepts of programming in a high-level language

REFERENCE

JENSEN, KATHLEEN, and WIRTH, NIKLAUS (1975). *Pascal User Manual an
Report*, Springer-Verlag.

This is the definitive document for the programming language Pascal, use
in this book.

THEORY OF COMPUTATION

KORFHAGE, ROBERT, R. (1966), *Logic and Algorithms, with Applications t
the Computer and Information Sciences*, John Wiley and Sons.

A sound readable introduction to the theory of algorithms, sets, boolea
algebra, and logical calculus.

Pascal language summary

B.1 VOCABULARY

The set of basic symbols in Pascal consists of *letters*, *digits*, and *special symbols*. The special symbols may be classified into *operators*, *delimiters*, and others.

B.1.1 The letters

A...Z, a...z

B.1.2 The digits

0 1 2 3 4 5 6 7 8 9

B.1.3 The operators

arithmetic operators:	+ − * / **div mod**
set operators:	+ − *
boolean operators:	**or and not**
relational operators:	= <> < <= >= > **in**
parentheses:	indexing brackets [ ]
	expression brackets ( )
	comment brackets { } (* *)
	statement brackets **begin end**
assignment operator	:=
quote mark	'
pointer symbol	↑

B.1.4 Delimiters

statement separators:	**if then else case of with**
	while do repeat until for to downto
other separators:	. , : .. ;
specifiers:	**const type var procedure function**
	array packed file record set program

B.1.5 Other special symbols
the null pointer: **nil**
jump operator: **goto**
label declarator: **label**

B.1.6 Identifiers
The following class-names for objects which occur in the syntax rules are all
defined as identifiers:

type-identifier	procedure-identifier
variable-identifier	control-variable-identifier
field-identifier	
function-identifier	
file-identifier	
constant-identifier	

B.1.7 Standard identifiers
constants: *false true maxint*
types: *boolean integer char real text*
file-identifiers: *input output*
functions: *eof eoln odd chr ord pred succ abs round trunc arctan
                  cos sin exp ln sqr sqrt*
procedures: *get put reset rewrite read write readln writeln page
                  pack unpack new dispose*

B.1.8 Identifier syntax
identifier = letter {letter | digit};

B.1.9 Constants syntax
(The oblique stroke symbol '/', is equivalent to the vertical bar, '|', which it
replaces in the following syntax rules.)

constant	= [sign] unsigned-number
	/ [sign] constant-identifier
	/ string ;
sign	= "+" / "−" ;
unsigned-number	= unsigned-integer
	/ unsigned-real ;
unsigned-integer	= digit {digit} ;
unsigned-real	= unsigned-integer "." unsigned-integer
	/ unsigned-integer ["." unsigned-integer]
	"E" [sign] unsigned-integer
unsigned-constant	= unsigned-number
	/ string

                    / constant-identifier
                    / ```"nil"``` ;
string   = ```"'"``` character {character} ```"'"``` ;

Constant

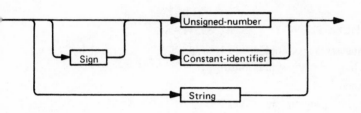

Unsigned-number

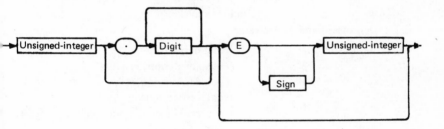

Unsigned-integer

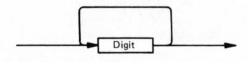

Unsigned-constant

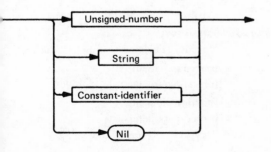

String

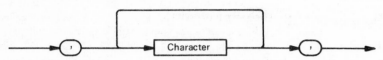

B.2 BNF DEFINITION OF PASCAL SYNTAX

(The oblique stroke symbol, '/', is equivalent to the vertical bar, '|', which it replaces in the following syntax rules).

B.2.1 Program

    program = "**program**" identifier
          "(" file-identifier {"," file-identifier} ")" ";" block "." ;
    file-identifier = identifier ;
    block   = definitions-and-declarations
               compound-statement ;

B.2.2 Definitions-and-declarations

    definitions-and-declarations = [label-declaration-part]
                    [constant-definition-part]
                    [type-definition-part]
                    [variable-declaration-part]
                    [procedure-and-function-declaration-part] ;
      label-declaration-part   = "**label**" unsigned-integer
                          {"," unsigned-integer} ";" ;
      constant-definition-part = "**const**" constant-definition
                          {";" constant-definition}";" ;
      constant-definition   = identifier "=" constant ;
      type-definition-part   = "**type**" type-definition
                          {";" type-definition} ";" ;
      type-definition   = identifier "=" type ;
      variable-declaration-part = "**var**" variable-declaration
                          {";" variable-declaration} ";" ;
      variable-declaration   = identifier {"," identifier}":" type ;
      procedure-and-function-declaration-part
                        = {procedure-declaration/function-declaration
      procedure-declaration   = "**procedure**" identifier
                        [formal-parameter-list] ";" block ";" ;
      function-declaration   = "**function**" identifier
                        [formal-parameter-list]
                      ":" type-identifier ";" block ";" ;

```
formal-parameter-list    = "(" formal-parameter-section
                           {";" formal-parameter-section} ")" ;
formal-parameter-section = parameter-group
                         / "var" parameter-group
                         / "function" parameter-group
                         / "procedure" identifier {"," identifier} ;
parameter-group          = identifier {"," identifier}
                           ":" type-identifier ;
```

B.2.3 Type

```
type = simple-type
     / ["packed"] structured-type
     / pointer-type ;

simple-type      = scalar-type
                 / subrange-type
                 / type-identifier ;
scalar-type      = "(" identifier {"," identifier} ")" ;
subrange-type    = constant ".." constant ;
type-identifier  = identifier ;
structured-type  = array-type
                 / record-type
                 / set-type
                 / file-type ;
array-type       = "array" "[" simple-type
                   {"," simple-type} "]" "of" type ;
record-type      = "record" field-list "end" ;
field-list       = fixed-part [";" variant-part]
                 / variant-part ;
fixed-part       = record-section {";" record-section} ;
record-section   = [field-identifier {"," field-identifier}":" type] ;
variant-part     = "case" [field-identifier ":"]
                   type-identifier "of" variant {";" variant} ;
variant          = [case-label-list ":" "(" field-list ")"] ;
case-label-list  = constant {"," constant} ;
set-type         = "set" "of" simple-type ;
file-type        = "file" "of" type ;
pointer-type     = "↑" type-identifier ;
```

B.2.4 Expression

```
expression = simple-expression [relational-operator simple-expression] ;
simple-expression   = [sign] term
                    / simple-expression adding-operator term ;
```

```
        term                   = factor
                               / term multiplying-operator factor ;
        adding-operator        = "+" / "−" / "or" ;
        multiplying-operator   = "*" / "/" / "div" / "mod" / "and" ;
        factor                 = variable
                               / unsigned-constant
                               / "(" expression ")"
                               / function-designator
                               / set
                               / "not" factor ;
        function-designator = function-identifier [actual-parameter-list] ;
        function-identifier   = identifier ;
        actual-parameter-list = "(" actual-parameter {"," actual-parameter} ")" ;
        actual-parameter       = expression
                               / variable
                               / procedure-identifier
                               / function-identifier ;
        set                    = "[" [element {"," element}] "]" ;
        element                = expression / expression ".." expression ;
```

B.2.5 Variable

```
    variable = variable-identifier
             / component-variable
             / referenced-variable ;
        variable-identifier   = identifier ;
        component-variable = indexed-variable
                           / field-designator
                           / file-buffer ;
        indexed-variable    = array-variable "[" expression {"," expression} "]" ;
        array-variable      = variable ;
        field-designator    = record-variable "." field-identifier ;
        record-variable     = variable ;
        field-identifier    = identifier ;
        file-buffer         = file-variable "↑" ;
        file-variable       = variable ;
        referenced-variable = pointer-variable "↑" ;
        pointer-variable    = variable ;
```

B.2.6 Statement

```
    statement = [label ":"] unlabelled-statement ;
        label                = unsigned-integer ;
        unlabelled-statement = simple-statement
```

```
                              / compound-statement
                              / conditional-statement
                              / repetitive-statement
                        ·     / with-statement ;
    simple-statement       = [assignment-statement
                              / procedure-statement
                              / goto-statement] ;
assignment-statement = variable ":=" expression
                              / function-identifier ":=" expression ;
    function-identifier    = identifier ;
    procedure-statement = procedure-identifier [actual-parameter-list] ;
    procedure-identifier   = identifier ;
    goto-statement         = "goto" unsigned-integer ;
    compound-statement = "begin" statement {";" statement} "end" ;
    conditional-statement = if-statement
                              / case-statement ;
    if-statement           = "if" expression "then" statement
                              ["else" statement] ;
    case-statement         = "case" expression "of"
                              case-list-element {";" case-list-element}"end" ;
    case-list-element      = [case-label-list ":" statement] ;
    repetitive-statement   = while-statement
                              / repeat-statement
                              / for-statement ;
    while-statement        = "while" expression "do" statement ;
    repeat-statement       = "repeat" statement {";" statement}
                              "until" expression ;
    for-statement          = "for" control-variable-identifier
                              ":=" for-list "do" statement ;
    for-list               = initial-value "to" final-value
                              / initial-value "downto" final-value ;
    control-variable-identifier
                           = identifier ;
    initial-value          = expression ;
    final-value            = expression ;
    with-statement         = "with" record-variable
                              {"," record-variable} "do" statement ;
```

B.3 PASCAL SYNTAX DIAGRAMS

Program

Program

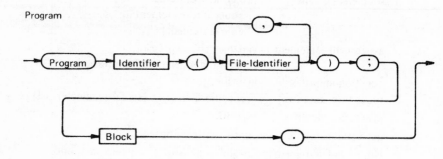

Block

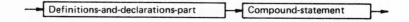

Definitions-and-declarations-part

Definitions-and-declarations-part

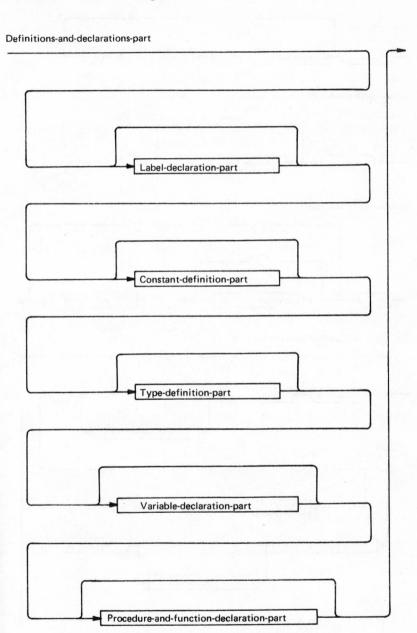

Constant-definition-part

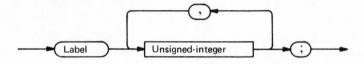

Label-declaration-part

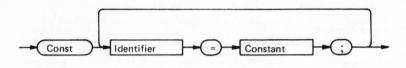

Variable-declaration-part

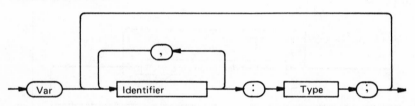

Procedure -and-function-declaration-part

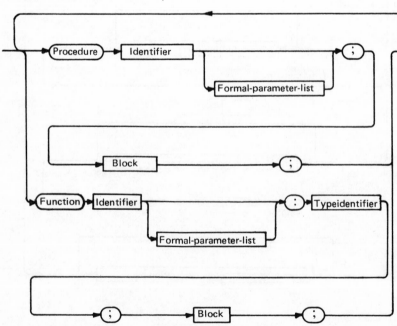

Formal-parameter-list

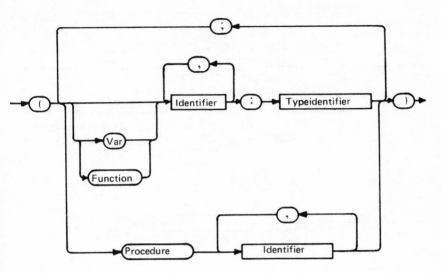

Type-definition-part

Type-definition-part

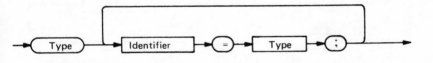

Type

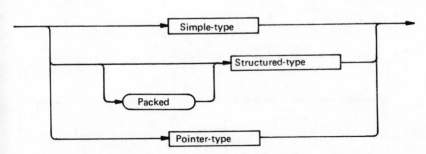

Simple-type

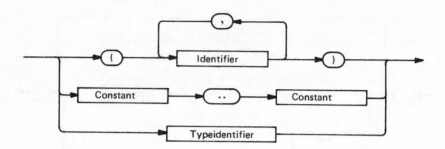

Pointer-type

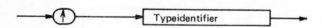

Structured-type

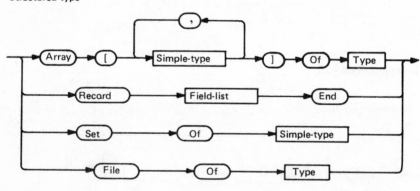

Field-list

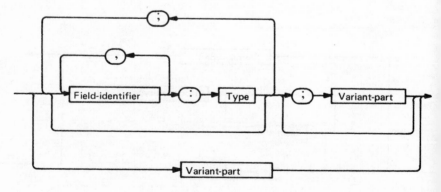

Variant-part

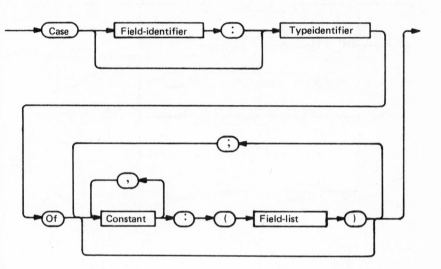

Expression

Expression

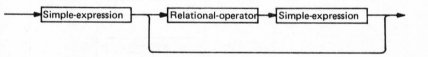

Simple-expression

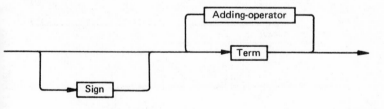

Term

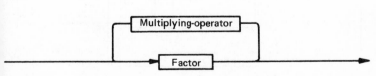

Factor

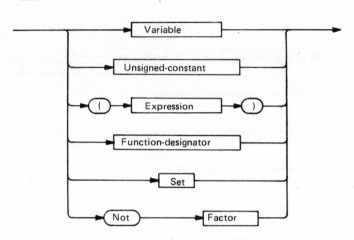

Function-designator

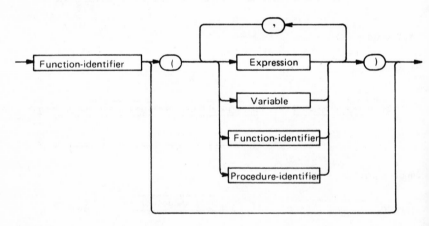

Set

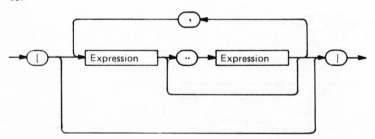

Variable

Variable

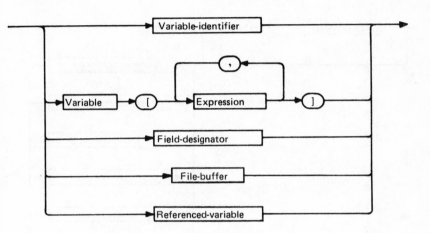

File-buffer

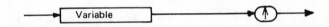

Field-designator

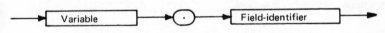

Referenced-variable

Statement

Statement

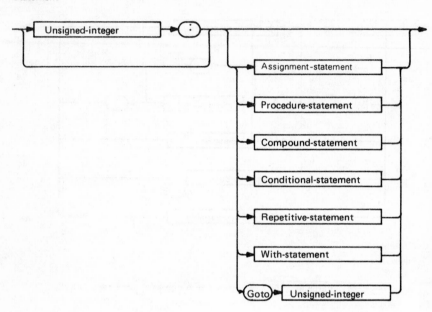

Compound-statement

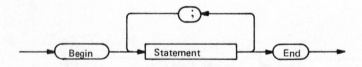

Assignment-statement

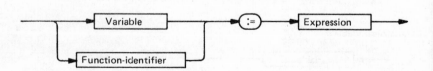

Procedure-statement

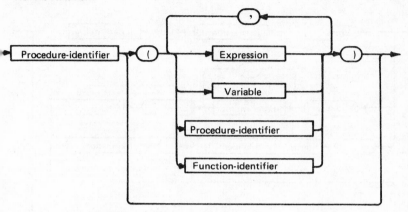

Conditional-statement

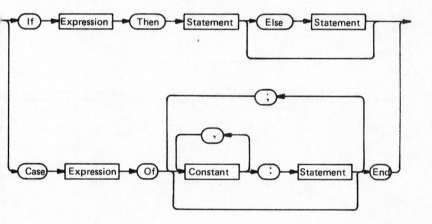

Repetitive-statement

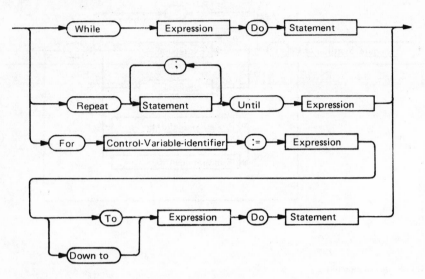

With-statement

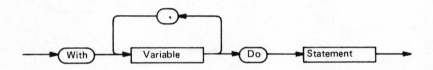

Index of programs and sub-programs

Subject Index